Black Power
A State of Mind
By O.C. Mather

September 2020

Black Power (is a State of Mind)

Introduction

For the first time in history, a Black Woman has been nominated to be the Vice President of the United States. She was nominated by a former Vice President who served under the first Black President of the United States. Within hours of her being named, the celebration started in many corners of the country as little Black girls began to smile and really understand what little Black boys already knew. We are intelligent and very capable people whose opportunities are limitless.

Black Power is some cool shit. Black Power is our haircuts, our style, our music, our dance, our ability to take spoken words and put them on a cool beat so that everyone dances around the world and can recite the words while they are outside of a car doing the latest dance. It is what makes us unique, gives us our individuality and while it may be copied, and at times mimicked, it can't be done the way we do it or did it. We are the originals of so many things and while many may try to take credit for some genre of something they are doing, it started with us.

We started singing in the church and ended up selling out arenas. Started creating things in the basement and ended up being on everyone's tablet. Started in the park and ended up in the Forum, the Garden, or at the Rucker. Started on the corner and ended up in the studio with sixteen bars. Yes, we are some cool ass people who do everything well. Once we learn it, we tend to master it. Just ask Tiger, Serena, or Lewis.

When you say the greatest of all time, do you think about Martin, Malcolm, Frederick, Muhammad Ali, Michael (Jackson or Jordan), Thurgood, Wilt, Denzel, Sidney, Lena, Aretha, Sheryl, Leslie, Deion, Magic, Chadwick or Lebron?

Black Power (is a State of Mind)

When you think of the coolest couples, is it Will and Jada, Denzel and Pauletta, Barack and Michelle, or Shawn and Beyonce? Or was it Ruby and Ossie, or Martin and Coretta, or Malcolm and Betty? Or could it be Courtney and Angela?

Coolest weatherman? Al, of course. Coolest dude to ever play a trumpet? Is it Louie, or is it Miles? Musical genius, Quincy, or Prince? I mean is there anything we can't do. Let's not forget the Tuskegee Airmen or Colin. Or Condoleezza. Definitely can't leave out Oprah, Maya, Nikki, Angela, Rosa, Barbara Jordan, or Shirley Chisolm. And let's not forget Jesse Jackson, Andrew Young, Vernon Jordan, Cory Booker, and John Lewis.

Writers who influenced generations and still do in Jimmy Baldwin, Richard Wright, Langston, Huey, Eldridge and Ta-Nehisi and Cornel, and Michael Eric Dyson. And W.E. Dubois and Booker T. Washington. There are many more Black men who wrote their truth for generations to come. They shared what resiliency looks like in the face of adversity. After a while we do it so well, we make the difficult look easy, and we turn pain into success. All the while, looking over our shoulder not for the next great one, but to make sure no one holds us back.

Black Power is all of the Black people who represent every profession in this country called America taking pride in their jobs whether they are the Neurosurgeon that separates conjoined twins to the maintenance man who brings power back to a building. They are the judges who help to enforce and ensure fairness in the law and the lawyers who fight for the freedom and rights of those who are innocent despite what the evidence may show. Black Power is so many things that have made us different, relevant, and able to survive when no one thought it possible.

Black Power (is a State of Mind)

Black Power is a state of mind. It is a way of doing things. It is style. It is our resiliency. It is confidence in one's abilities, it is uplifting each other, and helping each other to be our best us. It is that gift given to each of us by our creator to be the creative, intelligent, innovative, and artistic people that we continue to be.

This book is meant to do two things, uplift your soul and where appropriate call you on your bullshit. I can promise you if you read the entire book, and don't skim or gloss over it, you will find the Black Power you have been searching for all your life. You will find out that we can be our own oppressors by focusing too often on the negative stereotypes and trying to fit in at times in places where we are not wanted or at a very minimum made to feel as if we are not invited. Yet we are not giving ourselves credit for all we as a people have accomplished and will continue to accomplish. This book is not intended or to be confused with the Black Power movement of the 60's and 70's that had its own agenda and narrative.

We are in the middle of a pandemic and it has affected the Black community in ways we could not imagine taking loved ones far too soon and with no advance notice. Yet I am confident that this too shall pass knowing that it was a slave, a Black Man named Onesimus, who introduced the concept of inoculation to his slaveowner and ultimately it led to the eradication of smallpox, which was considered a lethal disease at the time. Yes, a slave, who may have helped to save more lives than can be counted over the last four hundred years with the introduction of a concept to the Americans of what was the precursor to the vaccine.

There are so many stories like this buried mind our history. I do not believe it is intentional that we don't learn about these Black American heroes in our history classes. I believe that we as Black parents need to make a concerted effort to teach our history to our children to enlighten them to the real possibilities that exist as shown and demonstrated by those who came before them and are still alive today.

Black Power is a mindset that has allowed us to survive coming over on a boat while being packed like sardines in less than humane conditions to a country that appeared to only want us for the free labor. Black Power is jumping off that same boat in the middle of the ocean and choosing to die a free man or woman while drowning in the middle of an ocean a martyr not knowing about a Heaven that would be introduced to enslaved people that promised an eternal life free of bondage, sickness or poverty.

Black Power is holding our heads up while our women were humiliated and harassed by their oppressors continually and without mercy. Black Power is loving a man who was taken away from his woman and his children not as a matter of choice but at the hands of his oppressor. The same oppressor would take his self-esteem away from him through constant torture and harassment, and at times sell him to the highest bidder to go breed other slaves much like we do animals today.

Black Power is surviving slavery if that makes any sense at all, being teased with freedom through reconstruction, and then being psychologically and physically enslaved again through another one hundred years of oppression by a shitty thing called Jim Crow. Black Power is having a strong will while looking down so that you don't make eye contact with a certain woman for fear of death through lynching or being spat on, kicked, chastised, hit with sticks, bats, and demeaned just because someone felt like it and it gave the oppressor a false sense of power thinking that they somehow had a hold of your mind and soul.

Black Power (is a State of Mind)

And the Black Power in you maintained self-control, did not act out or hit back because it was not time yet to let them know that you did not fear them, nor did you fear the inhumane treatment. What you feared was the gang like mentality that they exercised to try to control you. They controlled you on the outside, but you were only afraid of one man on the inside where it counted, and his name was GOD. You told them, but they would not listen.

They would listen soon enough. They would listen when you peacefully protested and you marched in suits and dresses, wearing your Sunday best and held the line all while being verbally harassed, and assaulted physically by those who were trying to demean you at every opportunity they could. You marched so future generations who so often scream about reparations could go to any school, buy a home, vote, and receive basic civil liberties and rights that should have been afforded to them the day they arrived in America like so many others who immigrated to this country, whether voluntarily or involuntarily in the case of the Black man, woman and child.

Black Power is refusing to go to war to fight against people who did you no harm to bring them civil liberties and rights that you could not get in your own country, even if it meant losing millions of dollars in endorsements and you had to relinquish your title like Muhammad Ali. Black Power is telling your coach, manager, or the owner that *"with the time I got left, I'm going to do it my way. Get my dollars up. You can trade me, waive me, or release me, but I will be worth 10 times what I was worth before I got here."* Because in the modern era, field hands get paid too. (A paraphrased line made famous by Jamie Foxx in the movie Any Given Sunday.)

Black Power is refusing to back down or be complicit when you see a peer get mistreated by a jealous boss who can't stand the fact that your peer and those like him or her are good at what they do, and instead of applauding them, he or she mistreats them out of fear that they will get their job. GOD forbid that they do well and actually make a difference in the organization because then that validates that it is not about the color of their skin, but instead the content of their character.

Black Power is having a limited education and becoming a best-selling author during the Jim Crow era like Richard Wright. Black Power is barely graduating high school, going to jail, and eventually becoming the leader of a powerful movement as well as a PhD like Huey Newton.

Black Power is being a comedian and realizing that shit ain't that funny when they laugh at you and not with you, so you walk away from a multi-million dollar deal like Dave Chapelle or transitioning from being just a comedian to becoming a bestselling author and civil rights activist like Dick Gregory.

Black Power is being free, but you keep going back to get those who are not free at much risk to your own life. Black Power is telling those you are trying to help gain freedom that there is no turning back and if you try to leave, you will get a bullet to the head. Now that is not only Black Power, that is bad ass. Her name was Harriet Tubman.

Black Power is getting up every day to go to a job that you do not necessarily like, to provide for your family while you pursue your dreams. Black Power is being a single mother who knows her true love is her children and knowing that her power resides not in wanting a man, or having a man, but instead making it happen somehow, someway every day. No, you as a single black mother don't need validation that you are a bad ass mom who doesn't take shit off anyone and will kill for her kids.

Black Power (is a State of Mind)

Black Power is Black males who don't quite fit perfectly into any situation because the world sees them as a threat, no matter how neat they comb their hair, or how professional they dress, nor does it matter if they speak the King's English or speak culturally like the neighborhood they grew up in. But then they still become President of the United States which is the biggest "Yes We Can" ever to all the oppression we as Black people have been through. No longer can we be looked down upon, or made to feel like three fifths of a man, because we just became one of forty-five of the most powerful men historically in the free world and in one historical vote all the myths about Black people not being good enough are invalidated.

When I first started this project, I was angry. I was angry because a man had just been killed by a man who was sworn to protect him. His killer who did not deserve to wear a blue uniform but instead should have been wearing an orange jumpsuit. His death was shown on national TV for the world to see and it was mind numbing to see a man kill another man (who happened to be Black) with no regard for human life and yet it was happening right in front of me. His name was George Floyd. Say his name.

George Floyd was a Black man who once ruled his high school with his personality and athletic ability. A brother to siblings, and a father to a beautiful little Black girl who loved her daddy unconditionally. I was angry because his life was taken for no reason at all other than the man who did it could take his life because he felt that he was above the law instead of enforcing the law. A knee to the neck for eight minutes and forty-six seconds that ignited a movement and made me sit down and rethink what mattered to me.

I continued to be mad, but then I began to realize that this man had not died in vain. And his death made him a martyr who resurrected a movement that had laid dormant for far too long. He reminded us all of who we, as African Americans, are as a people. We are a proud group of people who fear no man, take shit from no one, and have never felt inferior to anybody walking this earth. We are a proud people who have survived slavery, Jim Crow, overt, covert, systemic and right in your face racism. We have survived poverty, harassment, false incarceration, and cruel and unusual punishment.

We have survived while not having an identity that we can trace beyond a boat ride that broke the chain of our ancestry so that we will never know our true roots and who we are as a people both individually and collectively. We continue to survive even while facing ongoing and continuous adversity that comes with the uniform we wake up with every morning. In sports, you suit up to go out and face the competition. Well, our suit is our skin color and we suit up every day to first, stay alive, and then beyond that to keep moving forward so that we don't give up on the one man who has had our back from the very beginning and that is GOD, also known as Allah throughout the world to my people as well.

So, to all the powerful Black sisters and brothers who make up an immensely powerful group of people that have been something to reckon with for over 400 years in this country we call America, I salute you. You are some bad ass individuals who keep on keeping on, never looking back, but never forgetting. You have shown forgiveness where frankly it is not always deserved and most importantly, you love people who despise you and in some cases hate you not because you are a bad person or have harmed them in some way, but simply because you hold your heads up high, keep trying, and persevere despite the odds. The very fact that we wake up every day not wanting to just scream is a testament to the fact that we are great people and that is because of our Black Power.

My goal is to tell you about our Black Power by highlighting all that is great about you. We can win, and we are winning. We can get our reparations, and we are getting our reparations. We can learn, and we are learning. What we need is a focus on who we are, what we as a people are capable of, and how we exercise our rights as Americans to maximize our potential, our capabilities, and all that we have to offer not this country, but the world itself. As we have done for the past 400 years and throughout history.

We are not inferior people, nor are we superior to anyone. We are not GOD. What we are is some bad ass brothers and sisters who kick ass and take names. We can walk the walk and talk the talk. It's a mindset that we must recapture and reclaim in order take back all that matters to us, and that is our GOD given talents and abilities to own our own businesses, have creative control and ownership of everything we do, control our destinies, and stop trying to emulate behaviors that won't get us the acceptance that so many of us continue to seek. We should never want to emulate anyone, regardless of their race, or background who would rather find fault in you rather than focus on themselves.

In the meantime, get your life together, get your education, keep improving and growing, marry you a fine piece of chocolate (male or female) and make beautiful babies to keep Black Power alive. And Morgan Freeman was right, we do not need a Black History Month, we are history, period and a people that should be read about, talked about, celebrated, and thought of 365 days of the year. Stop letting people who may not have your best interests at heart dictate what you learn, worship, celebrate, believe, and enjoy. Black Power. A State of Mind.

For 2 Long

If for one day, I could sit at a table,

Break bread and talk to the men and women for whom I am most inspired,

The ones who never rested, and despite the physical and mental fatigue felt no ways tired.

If I could just listen and hear what they had to say,

It would further confirm my faith and why I pray.

For you see these people represent all that I am and all I aspire to be.

Because for as long as they tried, they understood freedom ain't free.

They tried by any means necessary, were falsely convicted of crimes.

They spoke their truths and withstood the test of time.

Legacies, poets, artists, and leaders them all.

None failed, all succeeded, despite the haters and critics who wanted them to fall.

Endurance, stamina, they sacrificed everything for you and me.

We might not know full freedom, but they helped to make you free.

Do things differently, I doubt they would say that in hindsight,

And that is my truth as well, and that is why I write.

O.C. Mather

Allow Me to Introduce Myself

The Black Power movement and other similar activities were birthed in the 1960's during a time when we as a people were trying to fight systemically on many fronts to recognize our suffering, identify our needs, and try to come up with solutions to address those needs. Not a want, but a need. Ironically, many of the people and these organizations that were part of these movements have since died or the organizations disbanded. And to date no modern organizations have realized the level of resurrection that gave these disbanded organizations such a high profile that the government felt it necessary to monitor them. The saddest thing about that, is that the people and leaders who were being monitored simply wanted a better life for themselves and the people who looked like them than they had been able to achieve previously during slavery and the Jim Crow era. They were honoring those generations that came before them by attempting to hold the system and America accountable and attempting to pay it forward for those who would come after them.

Rather than keep the momentum going, these organizations were infiltrated, dismantled or had some rogue member within them who were part of a divide and conquer mentality that was a learned behavior taught to us by our oppressors during slavery that continues to haunt us to this day. There will be people who will try to find fault in this book. They will try to discredit it as an opinion-based narrative that has some agenda to do more harm than good. You will always have critics and naysayers when you are telling the truth.

They may come from the left, the right, and the center. And sadly, some of them will look like me. Instead of finding what is good about this book, and taking a couple of golden nuggets that will help them to understand what Black Power is to move the needle for us all, they will instead try to convince others there is no Black Power and no need for Black Power, and that we need to fit in where we can get in, and do what folks tell us to do. That is a mentality that has no race or demographic assigned to it, but is the prerequisite to not having a mind of your own and seeing this book for what it really is, a narrative on having freedom and autonomy to exercise the Power we have in us to be all we can be. But I digress.

When I think of Shawn "Jay Z" Carter, I see many things. I see the Black brother who paved his own way, did it the way he wanted to, was not beholden to anyone, and did not sacrifice his identity to acquiesce or appease some board of directors or to meet a status quo. He spits or raps his truth, unfiltered and without apology to anyone. That is what I have admired about him the most as I have been a fan for many, many years. There are those who will criticize some, if not all of his raps for the lyrics, the profanity, and other things, but you can't criticize the business model or the work he has done in his later years to give back and pay it forward.

Jay Z's influence on this project is shaped by his ability to make his own music when no one would sign him to a deal. It is my belief that if you put out a good product, and it can generate the appeal of the right readers, then you should do it yourself and own your property.

So rather than spend time on who I am (pointless) or talk about all my success (six figures or more annually since I was thirty years old), I will simply say this. If you need to know who I am, and where I went to school, and how many parents I have (one, two, or step), then this book is not for you. It simply means you have the mentality of someone who is more concerned about my "street cred" as they call it or the lack thereof then you are about getting the years of experience and knowledge that I am sharing with you. I have made more money in my lifetime than I care to talk about, and it did not make me happy. I have owned and lived in two homes at one time. I have lived in the mountains, a block from the beach, in the big city, and currently reside in a big town as they call it in the south.

Cars, I have had plenty, and back in my day, I enjoyed life to the fullest in this material world that we call home and America. None of that means much to me anymore because I would rather have Black Power than be powerless in a world that seems to value materialism, power, and fame more than being a difference maker and a change agent.

Black Power to me is about having the power, not the titles. Having the power to change the world through the stroke of a pen, the keys on a keyboard, being able to jump higher and farther, run faster, or create the next app that inspires others to chase their dreams and freedom as well. Black power is controlling your own destiny by being fiscally responsible so that if you have to work or just like to work for others, one day you can retire and live the rest of your life on your own terms. Black power is about saving lives, and mentoring the next generation by sharing your experiences, both good and bad, to help them navigate this thing called life.

Work ethic cannot be taken away from you. Education once received cannot be taken away from you. Your past accomplishments and failures that you learned from cannot be taken away. And that is your Black Power. Manage your life in a way that nothing can be taken away from you once earned. You always can get another job, another house, and another car. You can rebuild your credit. But your successes, once achieved, can never be taken away from you.

Black Power (is a State of Mind)

So, spend no time worrying about who wrote this, or who I am, or where I come from. Spend time learning and digesting and reflecting so that you can reclaim your Black Power. My background and what I did or do for a living does not take away from the information being shared and the knowledge you will receive.

Much like Shawn Carter, also known as Jay Z, allow me to introduce myself and allow me to reintroduce you to the Black Power that is within you. The Black power that is screaming to get out, and do great things, invent the next iPhone, develop the next vaccine, or create sixteen bars that tell your story and uplifts another brother or sister to conquer the world.

"If I could have convinced more slaves

that they were slaves,

I could have freed thousands more."

Harriet Tubman

Why Now?

The preceding saying by Harriet Tubman speaks volumes on the mentality of African Americans during slavery and to a great degree, even now in the 21st century. Many of us will not chase our dreams, and we will make every excuse under the sun for why we are not ready, or it is not the right time. But if not now, when?

Harriet Tubman escaped slavery and the institution of slavery and secured her own freedom and yet she sacrificed and was able to go back over ten times to bring others to freedom. It is said that if anyone tried to stop or turn back, she would make them an offer they could not refuse. They could move forward, or she would kill them on the spot. It is said that she never loss one slave to desertion for the entire time that she led the Underground Railroad.

Now you might ask why anyone would follow this woman who keeps coming back to help others to freedom? Why would this Black female Moses spend so much time plotting and planning to help others who looked like her escape to freedom. Could it be Harriet had nothing to lose?

Well except for Harriet Tubman who kept putting herself at risk and if captured would probably have been killed on the spot, the other slaves had nothing to lose. Theirs was not a life worth living. Poor diet, no benefits, a job that required a lot of labor for no compensation in return, and at the end of the day, you could be sold to the highest bidder and not know if the conditions you were going to would be worse than your current conditions, if that was even possible. Let us not forget the fact that if you did not meet your production goal as it related to picking cotton, you could be whipped just for missing your weight count by a couple of pounds. If the expectation was you pick 400 pounds of cotton in a day, you might be punished severely for coming in at 398 pounds despite the fact another slave, who we would call a peer today, might have picked 450 pounds.

What I am saying is if people that came before you could live in those conditions and somehow survive it to produce generations that ultimately led to your own birth as a Black person, how can you make a difference in this world for yourself and those who look like you? If Harriet Tubman could exercise her Black Power to free slaves from bondage at great risk to her life, how can you become a difference maker today? That is the point of Black Power being a state of mind.

Showing loyalty to those that do not value you or your talents is not in your best interest. It typically causes more harm by stagnating your future and is the equivalent of being stuck in quicksand and just waiting to sink deeper. We all have choices. We need to make different choices about life. That is where the Black Power in all of us resides. Remember, you have nothing to lose. It is critical that we adjust our mindset to be winners, not losers. No situation is exempt from this thought process.

I love it when someone tells me I do not understand. I cannot help but ask what it is I am not understanding. "You are an educated Black man." I was not always educated. I had to learn. "You have had good breaks in life." I have had some failures as well. "People like you, and they give you opportunities." No, I earned them based on my work ethic and motivation to be better today than I was yesterday. "I do not want to leave my area code." Seriously? If your area code has a high crime rate, a high unemployment rate, and there are no opportunities to succeed that are legal, and provide future opportunities, you may be in the wrong area code.

Black Power (is a State of Mind)

I am not advocating abandoning home or forgetting where
you come from, but I am advocating abandoning a sinking
ship. You know the difference. History has taught us the
difference. We did not migrate North and West because we
wanted to ski or surf. We did it for the opportunities. You
may come back to that area code one day and potentially
make a difference, but you must act now to improve your
circumstances and sometimes that requires leaving home to
make a new home.

James Baldwin, Quincy Jones, Richard Wright, and W.E.
Dubois to name a few left the country to go where there were
opportunities to be free and treated like men. Not Black men,
but men. Quincy eventually returned. They went where they
could be receive the same respect as their peers who did not
look like them. Why did they do it? They had nothing to
lose. So, if they could leave the country, surely you can leave
an area code to find opportunity.

So again, what do you have to lose? Harriet Tubman. Black
Power. Those who followed her. Black Power. Approaching
life differently with a nothing to lose attitude. Black Power.
Moving where the opportunities are. Black Power.

What happens to a dream deferred?

Does it dry up

like a raisin in the sun?

Or fester like a sore--------

And then run?

Langston Hughes

Black Power (is a State of Mind)

Don't be the Angry Negro

When Martin Luther King gave his speech at the March on Washington some 50+ years ago, the line "I Have a Dream" resonated with so many African Americans and for one day, gave them hope that change was coming. Change did come through efforts that helped to create the Civil Rights Act of 1964, the Voting Rights Act of 1965, and the Fair Housing Act of 1968. And from those three acts of law and others that preceded them in years past, African Americans were able to go out into the world and finally feel what one might call real freedom. I have equal rights, no more drinking from a different water fountain. I can vote for the best candidate who has my best interests at heart, and I can live anywhere I want. Like George and Weezie on the TV show, I can move on up.

But hold up, wait a minute! I am still poor, living below the poverty line, and the wages I am being paid do not allow me to escape my surroundings which are not an indicator of the freedom I have been seeking forever. And what about the voter suppression, and folks trying every trick in the book to keep me from voting. Move the polling place, not enough voting booths, need my ID, do not need my ID, planning to have police at the polls. And then there is this thing called gentrification.

Oh, and let us not forget the census and ensuring that we include and exclude where possible to redraw the lines to control the votes gained to enforce the laws that were passed in the 60's. I mean, come on, you sold me the car. Do I get to drive it or not? If not, then give me my money back and I will go somewhere else. Wait, I cannot get my money back because you are the only car dealership in town, America. I either take the car as is or I have no car at all. Okay, I will take the car, we will worry about an engine later. And yet I continue to love this country called America as does most, if not all of Black Americans.

This is not an agenda on how bad or good America is. America is the greatest country in the world. It is instead a narrative on the real possibilities of what freedom can be and how we as a people are searching in all the wrong places for that which we really desire, and that is our utter and complete freedom. We need that freedom so that we do not become pessimistic, complacent, and apathetic individuals who see no reason to vote, try, or even care anymore. We don't want to do the minimum required without having done our best. When that happens, we lose our ability to go forward and our Black Power is no more and well frankly, we are just listless people floating through life waiting to die.

I have witnessed this all too often within my own family and friends. And I have had the unfortunate reality of it happening to me. For everything that has been successful about my life, there have been situations where people who did not look like me made it a point to remind me that I am a Black man and to "know my place", "know my role" and "stay in my lane". How did they do this? I am glad you asked.

Let us look at the example of one of the first jobs I had after leaving college. What I did does not matter, nor is it important to name the type of industry I worked in. What is important is to recognize when someone is trying to bring out the worst in you to ruin you, your career, and your ability to provide for your family. I will remember this moment for the rest of my adult life and probably after I die, if you listen to my wife who says I will not let it go.

Black Power (is a State of Mind)

Early in my career, one of the first jobs I had was in the lending business. I was at work, and I knew that another employee was doing something that was not ethical and was putting the office at risk. In that office at the time, there were five of us. No one looked like me, as would be a common theme as I moved through the ranks ultimately becoming a vice president for a Fortune 500 company. I brought my concern to the attention of my manager at the time and told him that something was not quite right. He listened but blew it off as nothing. The next month, same thing, she is up to something and now I can prove it as I have noticed a pattern of behavior where she does not want anyone to manage certain accounts that are assigned to the branch and I know which accounts they were.

I brought it to the attention of my manager once again, and then he said something that was beyond comprehension. He said to me "You know back in the day they were hanging people; you would have asked for a new rope". He said it without hesitation and with no remorse and no apology to me. Now, I had two choices, become angry and lash out or react in a calm manner. I said, "excuse me" and he repeated it again. Up until that point, he had appeared to be a straight up guy whose demeanor towards me was nothing but professional.

What my boss at the time was doing was trying to put me in my place. This was in the late eighties, but had it been thirty years earlier, I might have had to leave town not knowing how to interpret his lynching comment. When I brought it to the attention of those in positions of power to look into it, the only outcome was that he did not mean what he said, and other than that, had I had any other incidents with him. Of course, the answer was no. But who hangs (no pun intended) around after something like that is said, you report it, and nothing is done? It was at that point, that I decided I had two choices. I could be a field hand, or I could be a boss, the boss of me. Black Power.

(Note: The young lady that I suspected of doing something shady was eventually caught committing fraud against the company. I would suppose that the reason no one believed she was doing anything was because well, how could she?)

For African Americans, we must know what our Kryptonite is and avoid it at all costs. Superman had one vulnerability, and that was Kryptonite. It zapped all his strength and made him a mortal again. And mere mortals are not superheroes. We as African Americans are superheroes. What we must do though, is not let people control how we act, think, and carry ourselves. I was angry that day the comment was made about the rope, but I did not show it.

What was most frustrating about that incident was that it was my first welcome to the real world after graduating from college. There will be those who say you let that one thing get to you like that, and my answer would be I sure did. The fact that he said it out in the open without hesitation in front of the other three employees in the office meant he felt he was superior to me and I was the inferior individual who had to just take it. I learned something else that day but did not know it at the time as it hit me many years later in my career after more incidents like that. We must 1) control our anger and we should 2) always be chasing our freedom.

The slaves were freed but had no home or land to go to. In a lot of cases, they did not know where their families were given, they were relocated or sold all over the south and wherever slavery was practiced. Reconstruction came and was quickly overcome by Jim Crow and the Black Codes. Almost one hundred years later came the Civil Rights movement, but here we are today some fifty years later and for all the progress we have made to go another one hundred miles down the road to freedom, we have also gone twenty miles back over familiar terrain that we thought was long behind us.

We could be angry for so many reasons. Poor living conditions, the inability to save enough to leave those conditions, lack of empathy from those who continue to silently and stealth-like oppress us every day, lack of opportunity or the stagnation of opportunity when we finally get an opportunity to join a company and get what some call a "good job", and then there is the food deserts, the inadequate or lack of a healthcare systems in some pockets of the country, the entitlement myth and urban legend that we don't want to pull our fair share.

The irony of the "pull our load" comment is ironic and comical because if not for Black people, this country would not have been built, period. This country prospered and became great on the backs of African Americans long gone who were beaten, raped, separated from their families, tortured, mutilated, forced to eat things that were not fit for consumption. Slaves were forced to live in conditions that were less than what a dog received during a time when we were thought of as barbarians and savages simply because the owners wanted them to believe that they were the problem.

While anger can be our Kryptonite, throughout history, we have tried to find a way to turn the other cheek and be a forgiving people based on the "Good Book" that taught those very principles and was taught to us by the very people who did not think enough of us to make us ever feel wanted in a country that belonged to none of us but instead belonged to a people who were chased off their land (Native Americans) to allow others (Colonizers) to take it over and then enslave a group of people (Black People) to work the land and build this country.

And yet somehow, we try extremely hard not to be angry. To this day, all that we ask for is the ability to succeed and be treated fairly by the definition of doing what is right. It is ironic that when it was time to go fight the last world war (WWII), it was expected of everyone to participate and do their fair share as America had everything on the line. African Americans did that with pride for a country that would assign them back to a caste system when the war was over.

When African Americans returned from World War II, they were told that the G.I. Bill only applied to veterans who did not look like them. Some veterans could buy a home, African Americans could not. My father was one of those veterans. Locked out of the first step to generational wealth for no reason other than the color of their skin. And yet, the anger was managed, and the attitude of "that is just the way it is" was developed. So then comes the pessimism, the complacency and the apathy towards life that if not checked, leads to a numbing of the emotional and mental state of the African American that may look like laziness that does not exist but why work hard if you dangle the carrot, but only provide the stick, both physically and mentally?

But then there is that thing called freedom, and that is why I love America. Freedom is having the resources to be beholden to no one. It begins with understanding all the things that deny you the freedom that you are so abundantly seeking. Real freedom requires real sacrifice and it is those sacrifices that have kept African Americans from exercising the Black Power needed to achieve that freedom. What are the things that deny you freedom? I am glad you asked.

The things that deny you freedom are not overly complex to understand. It is the things that require your money, your time, your energy, or keep you coming back and only satisfy wants, not needs. It is the people who hold you back, stifle your creativity and bring drama to your life. It is the ability to believe in yourself and not listen to the haters, naysayers and trolls who desire to tell you how bad life is for you instead of focusing on their own circumstances.

It is the coworkers, peers, and bosses who see in you a threat to their own existence and spend every waking moment at work trying to sabotage your career through gossip, innuendo, and an all-out assault on trying to character assassinate you whenever and wherever possible. In today's America all it takes is an accusation to ruin a career and ruin your life.

And it can be your own family whose misguided jealousy and envy and a lack of understanding of the real world and our history causes them to mislead and misguide you by telling you that the world is not as it appears, and you should just look the other way, dumb yourself down, or do what them folks tell you to do.

This obsession with superiority and inferiority will be the thing that tears this country apart and ultimately leads us to our demise. It creates anger for people who regardless of their race are chasing the same thing, yet those in control communicate that it is a fair race but change the rules anytime they feel that certain individuals are starting to win. African Americans want to be treated fairly, love their neighbors, and pursue this "liberty and happiness" thing they have heard so much about while truly realizing the benefits. Black Power comes from our pursuit of this thing called freedom. Our Black Anger comes from being denied these freedoms when we play by the rules, and then the finish line is moved every time we almost break the tape to declare victory.

Be angry, but do not show it. Then your refusal to act up or lash out will confuse your agitators who want to cause you harm, be it mentally, physically, or emotionally. Never give those who want to see you fail the satisfaction of knowing your business, what you are going through, or being able to pass judgment on you because you hit a rough patch in life. Go to those you trust, develop a plan to rebound, and work that plan to get you back to normal. Whatever you do, don't get angry.

Now, what do we do to overcome this feeling of an unfair and uneven playing field? We suit up, play hard, and follow the rules differently. There was a boss who once who told a young man that a football field is 50 yards wide and 100 yards long. You can run down the middle or stay right on the edges of the out of bounds line. Just do not go out of bounds. It is time to run along the out of bounds line. And while someone is hoping you slip up, run that line like a ballet dancer and score that touchdown. And remember, never stay where you are not wanted, and always leave on your terms. Black Power. A state of mind.

The Black Power Project: Accountability in the 21st Century

By now I have peaked your interests, and you may have questions. You agree that we have nothing to lose, you agree that now is the time and you understand how to channel the angst and frustration of wanting to get ahead. And it is possible to succeed at the highest level in America. I know it is because I did it. The mindset of Black Power has nothing to do with titles, net worth, or being accepted by anyone that does not want to accept you for the King or Queen that you are. It is a way of life that must be taught and digested by every African American in these United States of America.

It works because it is not a new way of doing things, but instead a reminder of who we use to be, how we used to do things, and being successful not despite of each other, but instead because of each other. We need to be allies, and friends, and we need to be a community. A family of people trying to navigate an obstacle course that is ever changing as it has been for over 400 years. We need to know the rules, have them be out in the open for everyone to see, and not worry about who knows about them because you still need to put in the work.

Anybody can shoot a ball but there is only one Kobe, Michael, Magic, Shaq, or Lebron. Anybody can play an instrument, but there is only one Alicia, Miles, Duke, Coltrane, or Dizzy. Anybody can box but there is only one Floyd, Mike, Sugar Ray, Thomas, or Muhammad Ali. There is only one of every single person on this earth. There are no duplicates, no clones, and we all carry a unique DNA. And it is in that DNA that allow us to be unique to ourselves.

Our challenge, each and every one of us in the Black Community, is that we have to revive some simple things that have escaped us through frustration, loss of hope in some cases, and in a lot of cases, complacency and obsession with material things and a false belief that we are somehow winning a game that we can play, but has its own set of rules that can work for us or against us on any given day. But we have played this game for over 400 years, and here we are still on the field trying to win.

The best teams never quit no matter what the score is. History has shown us that losers can be winners when they learn what caused them to lose. Rather than take those losses as failures, they are turned into opportunities. Just ask anyone you know how they became winners, and they will tell you through failure. They shot the ball 9,000 times and only made 4,000 baskets. They swung at the ball 1,000 times only to hit it 300. They wrote that song ten times before it was a hit. They rushed the ball 30 times only to reach 120 yards in a game or 4 yards per carry. They invented the next great thing after trying to make it work many times previously. They built schools starting with one building and one foundation like Tuskegee University in Alabama. People have come before you and people will come after you who put in the work, came in early, stayed late, and made it happen despite the obstacles. But the key here is team. We need to be a team.

I wrote this book to redefine our Black Power and to lessen the psychological and mental dependency on some reparations that may never come, or some entitlements that we become so dependent upon that we don't put forth our best effort to first take care of ourselves and then take care of others who look like us. My **Points of Black Power** as I will call them will benefit you if you have an open mind, and are willing to change your way of thinking from barely making it, just trying to survive, and a false sense of winning to really winning. These points of power are simple:

- **Try GOD** and hold the Clergy accountable.
- **Read for Understanding** and know your history.
- **Master the Internet** and do not let the Internet be your Master.
- **Succeed despite the Odds.**
- **Buy Black** and bring back Black Wall Street.
- **Avoid the Shiny Shit,** no one really cares!
- **Reach One, Teach One** and create a legacy for generations to come.
- **Give Back** so those who are less fortunate can be givers themselves.
- **Teach Your Children** – their best teacher they will ever have is you.
- Politics in the Black Community **– Why we Vote!**
- **Uplift our Kings and Queens** – A letter to our future Kings and Queens!

Accountability:

an obligation or willingness to accept

responsibility or to account for one's actions

Try GOD

The concept of religion has always been a mystery to me. I have been baptized, joined more than one place of worship in my lifetime, and attended others or streamed them live. I was raised in a place of worship by two parents who were born in a time when on many days GOD was all African Americans had to lean on. To this day, I have questions, but I tend not to ask them too much because well, I was taught not to question my elders as a child, and lets' face it, GOD is the ultimate elder given his existence that predates the very creation of Earth.

What I have learned is that GOD (others may call him Allah), is important to understanding and properly channeling this thing called Black Power. It is impossible to walk outside and not understand who GOD is and see his incredible power at work. No matter what your current beliefs, there is one thing that you cannot deny, nor do you have an answer for. I mean think about it, how did all this get here? It was not through osmosis or some several thousand-years experiment that just got lucky. Why is there to my knowledge and yours no other planet that has life-forms on it like the planet Earth? Because I cannot explain how we got here and the incredible miracle of birth, I must attribute it to GOD.

It is also fair to understand why I struggle with the concept of some modern day places of worship that to me are just popcorn and cherry coke apparatuses with one goal in mind, and that is to get big enough to make the pastor/preacher famous, wealthy and powerful. That is not what one would have expected of Jesus or his disciples who were humble, meek men of little to no wealth. These places of worship in some cases entertain more than they teach and have lost sight of their real reason for existing, to do the Lord's work.

Black Power (is a State of Mind)

When a place of worship's leader has a home, whose value is worth five to ten times more than their average members home, and drive cars that cost as much as a member's house, then that is concerning. It is further concerning when the optics and perception is that the place of worship's leader is prospering on the backs of hard working individuals who frankly don't have it to give but give because they are reminded that giving is a requirement to help others and provide for the less fortunate. Places of worship should not be a business enterprise disguising itself as a non-profit entity doing work on behalf of GOD. Why is this so critical?

Because never has the place of worship been needed by so many seeking answers to unanswered questions related to life, living and the American way. This is true for African Americans because up until recent times and heading into the twenty-first century, the place of worship was a beacon of hope. When all else failed, we would put it in the hands of GOD. That is what I was told anyway. There is a reason they say Jesus is on the main line, tell him what you want.

African Americans cannot lose hope as that affects our ability to exercise our Black Power and have the right state of mind to push forward and be as great as we can be. When you put all your faith in a country that does not have a consistent history of taking care of the least of us or those who do not look like the majority of America, then you are putting your faith in the wrong place. The African American clergy have got to come together and be the voice of reason for the most marginally affected, disenfranchised, and all African Americans.

African Americans need hope, they need leadership, and they need spiritual guidance. Regardless of who wrote the Bible or how it has been interpreted from one generation to the next, it has concepts in it that do apply to living a life that is moral and ethical and provides a sense of pride and dignity that is the foundation of who we need to be as a people. Even an agnostic and an atheist can learn something through Proverbs, Psalms, and other books of the Bible. If I had read the book of Ecclesiastes in my childhood, and into my early adult life, it would have saved me from pursuing the wrong things and helped me understand my true purpose had nothing to do with material things, guilty pleasures, or titles of which none of those things will matter upon my death to determine if I have eternal life or suffer the damnation of Hell.

There will be those who are turned off by this chapter of the book because for whatever reason, they may not be able to grasp the concept of Try GOD. I understand and empathize with their reasoning, which is personal to them. I understand as I have questions about some aspects of religion that don't always necessarily align with what I see going on in the world, specifically as it relates to Black people as well as others whose plight seems to be one of always trying but never quite getting ahead.

But then I am reminded of my parents, and their parents and what GOD meant to them and how they shared that with me. That relationship with GOD keeps me in constant touch with my parents, and other GOD fearing relatives that I have lost through death over the years because much of what they taught me was inspired by their reading of the Bible, sermons of years gone by, and a foundation that can't be broken even when the house starts to collapse.

I once asked a lady who I found to be deeply religious why is there just a Heaven and a hell? I further asked if there were a place you could go after death if you were good most of the time and messed up some of the time. Her answer to me was surprising and enlightening. She said such a place did exist.

This was before I started to consistently read my Bible for clear understanding. So, I asked her where this great place was. Without hesitation, she said Earth. She shared with me that Earth was the place that you lived your life in such a way that your actions and the things you did would provide the resume of your life that determined whether you went to Heaven or hell. And there it was, a simple answer to what I thought was a deeply profound question.

There needs to be a sense of urgency in the Black community to bring the place of worship back to the forefront of leadership, a safe haven for folks to go to who are down on their luck, and a place of spiritual guidance that uplifts us as a people and provides the very foundation of who we used to be. GOD fearing, upright individuals who put GOD first. Putting GOD first drives our decisions about all the temptations placed before us in what has become a very perverse and materialistic world that is operating on a very loose foundation.

We, the Black community need to find our way back to places of worship. I believe there is a direct correlation to many of the social issues that exist within the Black community due to the absence of the places of worship in the daily life of African Americans.

You may have questions about today's Christianity and its place in our lives. I understand that men are less likely to go to places of worship than Black women and children, yet never has it been so important that we return to the place of worship. I am not here to pass judgement, but instead to ask that we return to the first place that became our escape from the harsh realities of life hundreds of years ago and continues to be our refuge to this day when all else fails. There is an equal amount of accountability required of both sides to implement what will be a challenging, but necessary initiative.

Black Power (is a State of Mind)

We have to give the places of worship a chance to embrace us and they need to embrace us all. And then we as members need to fulfill our obligation to attend places of worship and rebuild the Black community, one member at a time.

There is a story about a homeless man who went to a church early one Sunday morning. He had a long beard, his hair was all over the place, and he had on tattered pants, a shirt that was too small and a jacket that looked like it had seen its best days. He went and sat on the front row of the church so that he could get the full experience of the church and praise and worship with the rest of the congregation. On this particular Sunday, a new Pastor had been assigned and this was to be his first day at the church. Well, the Deacons and Elders of the church did not want the embarrassment of having the homeless man sitting in the front of the church and asked that he be removed. After some dialogue between the ushers and the homeless man, he agreed to move to the back of the church. As members filed into the church to see the new Pastor and hear him preach, they complained that the homeless man made them feel nervous. Given the members had some influence in the church as they were big tithers or givers to the church, the ushers asked the man to leave.

As the time drew nearer, everyone was in place and the choir had completed their spiritual. It was time for the Pastor to deliver the sermon. For some odd reason, he was not there yet. The Deacons and Elders were at a loss to where the Pastor was. But then out of nowhere came the homeless man. He walked down the aisle, past the ushers who were told to let him through so as not to cause a scene again, and he proceeded to walk to the front of the church. He removed what was a wig and fake beard. And to the surprise of everyone, it was the Pastor. The Pastor was the homeless man.

The Pastor went up on stage, grabbed a microphone and let's just say that what happened next was not for the faint of heart. He scolded the entire congregation, and the Deacons and Elders. He remined them that Jesus walked with everyone, not just a select few. He reminded them that the mission of the church was not to be some elite club whose membership had some predetermined criteria based on someone's appearance or status in the church. He further reminded them that the church was there for everyone because the church belonged to GOD. It was HIS house, and not the Pastor, the leaders of the church or those who gave the most money to build it. He also reminded them that they were treating less fortunate people (like the homeless man he portrayed) the same way they had been treated in the past by those who wanted to oppress them.

He ended church early and asked everyone to go home and think about what had happened that day. He challenged them to do some soul searching prior to returning to the church the next week. He further told them if he had to rebuild the church membership from scratch, he would do that as well. And he gave them an ultimatum that was a risk to him but the right thing to do. He told them that if they could not change their way of thinking about including everyone, and not just a few, then they could fire him understanding they would be confirming that this place of worship was nothing more than a country club requiring VIP membership for the chosen few. For him, that meant that this was not GOD's house but instead the Pastor's house and that he would not be a part of given the humility expected of him and the entire congregation.

There are exceptionally good Preachers doing great work all over America. They are making sacrifices, and doing everything in their power to live up to the expectations of their CREATOR to ensure that their congregations are properly cared for from the poorest member to the member who is able to provide more than most in the way of giving monetarily. I know of quite a few as I have traveled this country and taken a more active interest in religion. These religious leaders have been educated, mentored, and built great churches in some cases starting with one member.

There also needs to be some inclusiveness of Black clergy, regardless of denomination to form a coalition of leadership that can influence and push fairness and equality for Black people through the political process. Young people are trying to lead and drive change through peaceful protesting but in many cases, they don't have the access to the real leaders of the community, the most powerful, the wealthy and those in critical positions of leadership within the community and up to the federal level. Church leaders often have relationships and access to individuals who are the decision makers at all levels of business and the government.

This is critical to the Black Power movement for all African Americans. I can personally attest to being down, feeling depressed, or not knowing if a situation was going to work out. And then I fall back on the teaching of my parents, aunts, uncles, grandparents, and in-laws who were all church goers and things tended to work themselves out for me. My personal Black Power stems from knowing that if I put GOD first, then everything else will take care of itself.

There will be those who say I cannot believe in something that I cannot see or touch. Yet you cannot see or touch the wind, but you can feel it. That is a personal choice and it does not minimize your role and responsibility to be a strong Black person who understands that Black Power is a state of mind. I will only tell you that I went to church all my childhood until I graduated from college. Then I was agnostic for over twenty plus years. Then I joined the church and went through two of the toughest years of a thirty plus year marriage to the woman I am still married to. And without pause, I can tell you if not for GOD, I would not have been able to manage those two years while continuing to build that state of mind that gives me power. Black Power. A state of mind.

Black Power (is a State of Mind)

Read for Understanding

There is a joke, although not that funny when thought through in a serious manner, that if you want to clean up a bad neighborhood and get the criminals off the corners, just put a stack of books at each corner and all the criminals will leave. Reading is critical to everything that has to do with being successful in America. We must read for understanding, for ongoing success, for hope and to know who we are as a people from a historical perspective. Reading is a privilege given to us as Black people that we did not always have (during slavery) or necessarily embrace (during the Jim Crow era and in some cases even today).

When I was about six years old, my parents bought me a set of World Book Encyclopedia. Back then, my mother told me that reading was important and would open up the whole world to me. She was right.

The World Book Encyclopedia for an African-American kid from a small town in the South would open up the whole world to me both historically and from the standpoint of learning about the rest of the world and all the important people, both past and present who lived or had lived in it. That set of books would allow me to see the world differently and dream of being able to grow up one day and be a part of the world as a Black educated man, not just a man. I know we have the internet, but there is something about putting a book in my hands and turning the pages that is like no other learning experience in the world.

That love for reading would come and go over my school years only to resurrect itself when I had children and tried to pass on that same advice that my mother had passed along to me. I would buy books for my children and they both developed a love for reading, my youngest would read whatever he could get his hands on and my oldest first set of books would be the Goosebumps series. I believe he read every single book in the series.

That love for reading encouraged by my mother was increased tenfold by the amount of time my children spent reading. The ability to read and the love for reading had a true impact on their going to college. To their credit, they both received full academic scholarships.

What I find different today for so many people that I interact with and also observe via the media is a reliance on social media platforms to be their source of truth on many subjects. It could be politics, sports, or local gossip amongst friends. Rather than buy into some random posts and biased narratives on social media and network news that could on any day choose a side in favor of one party or the other, I prefer to read for myself and gather my own facts and thoughts to form my own opinions.

People, regardless of what political party their claim to belong to, always have something to say about the President, his party affiliation, and how his being elected into office is personally affecting them normally in some fabricated negative manner. Instead of going to the pity party with them, I want to know what the candidates stand for, in other words what is their platform?

And when one goes back and reads the results of the election, and understands that there were towns, cities and states where African-Americans chose to sit out the election rather than go vote, you lose that disappointment that he became President and understand that you should be disappointed in yourself if you did not vote. There is a correlation to not reading up on the candidates and the lack of knowledge about either candidate that leads to the outcome of elections.

Black Power (is a State of Mind)

Again, social media and the news outlets can't be your only sources of truth.

A black man of today who feels oppressed or affected by the events occurring in his modern era needs to only read his history to understand what he is going through may not be as bad as it appears or new to his generation. He simply needs to go back and read about Black History through the eyes of successful Black men from all walks of life who had come before him, many of them writers, educators, and activists who captured their history through their own writings like Richard Wright, Alex Haley, James Baldwin, W.E. Dubois, Eldridge Cleaver, Huey Newton, Dick Gregory and Booker T. Washington.

It was Alex Haley who I became introduced to when his highly acclaimed book, Roots, was brought to life on national TV for a full week by a young man named Levar Burton who played a slave named Kunta Kinte who was brought to America. We watched Kunta Kinte endure slavery and we watched him grow old and then we had the experience of watching this story as it moved through time telling the unfiltered story of Black America and all that Black people endured while trying to keep the family together and function in what was the Black community of our past. At that time, it was one of the most watched programs or series in television history.

I read books by these men so that I could understand what Black men before me had experienced to understand how serious the issues of my current environment really are, specifically the social unrest associated with the current justice system and racism, compared to what they had been through. And what I found was eye opening.

Black Power (is a State of Mind)

All of these men endured something that during their time seemed dreadful but was not as dreadful as the generation that preceded them. As you read them in historical order based on a point in time dating back over a hundred years, you begin to see things got a little better as time marched on. And that was encouraging for me despite the challenges we continue to have in this imperfect union we call America.

Booker T. Washington was born a slave but died a free man and the President of a university that exists today, Tuskegee. James Baldwin became an accomplished writer who is quoted by many writers, regardless of race to this day. And then there is Dick Gregory who was a comedian first, but became a prominent social activist trying to do what he could to affect change in the south during the Civil Rights movement.

The experiences of these great men through their own life stories and social interactions from the years of slavery up until the mid-seventies reminded me that what we were currently experiencing had similar comparisons to society's ongoing attitude towards Black men in America. It also reminded me that the Black man by virtue of his skin color is often treated either covertly or overtly as a second-class citizen relegated to mistreatment, being misunderstood, and socially expendable through a caste system that has existed for over 400 years. It can at times feel like the clock stops for the Black Man, but time keeps moving.

I also learned that we could do something about it as well. Booker T. Washington all but confirmed that in his book Up From Slavery by alluding to the fact that when you have something to offer society, well, society will embrace you and accept you as a productive member in good standing.

I also read books by Ta-Nehisi Coates, Cornel West and Isabel Wilkerson which allowed me to understand a more current view of America through a historical and current lens and well thought out writings about the racial issues and the status of the African American(s) of this country that still exist today.

In some cases it can feel like these writers continue to state the obvious, but then I began to realize that not only were they stating the obvious that Black people, while we were doing better in most if not all cases than our ancestors from just one generation removed, we are still dealing with some issues, that if left unchecked, can create challenges and obstacles for us, as a people. In other words, we have to continue to remix the same record through more modern writings to remind America that while much has changed, much remains the same.

Sadly, even after 400 years of progress in America from a manufacturing, educational, and technological standpoint, the Black man and woman continues to deal with oppression and his or her oppressor, be it the boss at work, the neighbor who does not want him in the neighborhood, or a justice system that is harsher to him than it is his counterparts in other races. Or so it seems.

And let us not forget to name a few of the great women writers and poets like Maya Angelou, Toni Morrison, Terry McMillan, and Nikki Giovanni and Angela Davis to name a few. These women have written books that allow black girls and women to see life from their perspectives. They too have withstood the test of time as being great Black writers with their gender having no bearing on their intellect or artistic abilities. They too have helped to shape the ongoing narrative of the experience of being Black in America.

Reading also gives me hope. The Bible is considered by many the greatest book ever written by man who did it supposedly through the inspiration of GOD. I say supposedly because the foundation of the Bible is solid. The interpretations over the years raise questions today because there are some parts of the Bible that do not quite match up with today's society.

And more importantly, it is no secret that the Bible and Christianity have been misused in some cases by those who have tried to control the Black man by convincing him that his circumstances, especially those that make him feel inferior or less than his counterparts in other races, is preordained.

The myth that Ham's viewing of his father Noah naked in his bed was the beginning of a permanent curse of Black people and ultimately was the root cause of their enslavement has to be challenged if in fact all men are created in GOD's image.

And then there are the business magazines, self-help books, health and fitness books, and all the other books that I have read over the years to make me a more well-rounded person trying to fit into a world that won't let you in if you can't talk the language of those who have the power and influence that you need to move your own agenda. There is a simple saying that reading is fundamental.

A high percentage of people stop reading when they graduate high school and a significant percentage of people stop reading books when they graduate college. What baffles me is when you look at the most successful people in the world, they all continue to read and read until the day they die. I cannot stress enough that you need to read everything you can get your hands on.

There is scene in the movie Good Will Hunting and Matt Damon plays a janitor at Harvard who is highly intelligent but only has a high school diploma. One night he is at a bar with his buddies, one of them played by his life-long friend and fellow actor, Ben Affleck and Ben is interested in a young lady, who attends an Ivy League school, at the bar. One of the male Ivy League students tries to embarrass Ben by demonstrating he is more intelligent therefore more deserving of the young lady's attention. Matt Damon's character becomes irritated and he intervenes on Ben's behalf. He tells the college educated young man that he is not who he thinks he is. And he (Matt's character) goes on to tell the Ivy League young man that he is nothing more than a plagiarizer and a privileged kid who thinks he's all that because he is paying over a hundred thousand and fifty dollars for an education to recite from books he has memorized rather than have his own thoughts. And to add a little more salt to the wound, Matt tells the young man that the same information can be acquired by getting simply going to the local library for some small change in late fees.

That is probably the most powerful scene in the movie. The point is that if you read consistently and diversify your readings, it will help you chase your dreams, know your history, and give you hope, that you can do anything. And you will never be intimidated by anyone, to include some highly educated schmuck who got the same education you can get by simply being the owner of a library card.

I will always advocate getting more education, but that is not always financially possible for everyone. One must remember that college degrees can't be taken away from you nor should we forget it was Dick Gregory who said in his autobiography titled *nigger* "that piece of white paper isn't enough unless they graduate you with a white face, too." His point, while very raw and unfiltered, was that the degree would not define you nor would it necessarily guarantee your success. So, you get the next best thing, a library card and invest in the books you love reading by slowly growing your own library. Reading is the key to life, a successful life.

And for the record, reading solely on social media platforms without fact checking the information is the absolute worst thing you can do. If you are not careful, you will be influenced by someone pushing their own agenda and trying to shape a bullshit narrative not founded on facts, but instead trying to get you to then share that misinformation to influence others. Do not do that. You will be complicit to spreading bullshit and it will grow more bullshit that once it starts spreading can affect people's lives through our political process, our faith process, and challenge the very faith you have in that which you have believed in all your adult life. Fact check and then double check that fact to make sure it is indeed a fact.

I love to read, my kids who are grown men now love to read, and my wife loves to read. For that reason, we are intellectually independent of each other and have interesting conversations about all types of subjects and can each bring a different perspective to the conversation. Not one of us is influenced by the other's readings unless it passes the "Bullshit Meter" test which means you are entitled to have an opinion on a subject, but it must be backed up with some learned knowledge of the issue you are discussing, debating or arguing given your own unique passion about that subject.

The next time you go to the mall to spend money on some material shit you don't need and may not be able to really afford (credit is not cash contrary to popular belief), go to the library instead or spend a fraction of that money on a good book. Reading is fundamental and it is also Black Power. A state of mind.

Black Power (is a State of Mind)

Note: By the way, in that movie, the young lady is so impressed with the highly intelligent janitor (Matt) with the high school diploma that she gives him her phone number. As he and his friends continue their night on the town, they see the smart-ass college kid later sitting in a diner. Matt's character sees him through the window and ask him does he like apples. The college educated kid has a dumb founded look on his face as to say well, yes, he likes apples. At that point, Matt's character slams a piece of paper against the window with the young lady's phone number on it and asks the gentleman "How do you like those apples? I got her phone number!" It is not always the guy with the most degrees who gets the girl. It is the guy who can read. Wait on it! Black Power. A state of mind.

Master the Internet, and don't let the Internet be your Master

When the internet initially took hold of America and the rest of the world, it opened up unlimited opportunities for so many people to have access to information that only a few had been privileged enough to have previously. It opened up the whole world to anyone who had a phone, tablet, or computer. And one may question on any given day if that is necessarily a good or bad thing.

It allows all of us to dream our own dreams in so many different ways. We can be in a museum in Paris right now or see the clear blue water of the tropics with such clarity that we actually think we can put our feet in the water and cool down. It allows us to have access to historical and academic information in the most rural and isolated parts of the world giving most of us equal access to the same information, in every corner of the world.

The internet has breathed life into society and brought us all together like no form of technology ever invented. To some degree, it is our Tower of Babel and yet it is also the answer to the Black man's prayers of hope and a fair chance at succeeding in life.

The Tower of Babel is an Old Testament story in the Bible that might be seen as symbolic when one thinks of the internet. The city of Babel in its time was known for its wealth, commercial trade, and splendor. The name Babel means "Confusion". When the people, who all spoke one language in the town of Babel came together, their intent was to build a city and a tower that would reach to the heavens.

The story reads that GOD was concerned that their intentions would result in an unintended consequence that allowed them to become so corrupted that they might bring about their own destruction. The Tower of Babel, if unchecked and mismanaged, would result in the potential demise of humanity. There are some who may look at the internet in that same way given the ethical and moral challenges it brings along with all the good it provides to humanity.

The internet has in fact created a universal language understood by everyone in the world. All coders speak the same language and the internet has been both a blessing and a curse to so many. A blessing to those who utilize it with balance and understanding of what a powerful tool it is. It has been a curse to those who would hijack it for materialistic, political or religious purposes at the expense of their fellow man to mislead and corrupt a society that is on its best day sometimes very fragile given all the information that inundates us through all the social media and news platforms that exist currently on the internet coupled with the 24 hour effect of never cutting off.

Then there is the constant and never ending streams of social activity, the ability to buy things at will, purchase the next big game only to get addicted to the upsells that come with getting to the next level of a game that only twenty years ago you paid one price and played until you mastered all the levels without the upsell. There is the pleasure impact of the instant pornography, and internet influencers who use their bodies instead of their minds to gain millions of followers that when researched, these same influencers make their entire income off the casual and addicted internet user who find that living vicariously through others or trolling them to no end is the answer to having no life of their own.

Our music has become so dependent on the internet that there is only mainstream music, not necessarily good music. Hip hop as well as other music genres is overly saturated by video streams, which can have the wrong influence if left unchecked and mismanaged. When the best we have to offer our generation of young influential future Black boys and girls is music influenced by streams and videos on the internet with the hopes that this too can be them, it is no wonder that we don't have more of them wanting to be academics, medical professionals, lawyers, and business leaders in their own communities. I mean why spend all that money on school when the fast buck is available via the internet.

Everyone is not an influencer. Everyone is not a rapper and frankly that insults the rappers of the past and present who take the craft profoundly serious regardless of the type of rap being produced, be it gangster, urban or mainstream (clean). But everyone with a microphone, a camera and a computer think they are an influencer. What is baffling to me is that they are paid enormous sums of money to push products to us as African Americans. And often this is done by companies that we have no ownership interest in, don't sit on the board of directors, or have any influence on what products they are selling or their impacts to our communities. We have to do better.

I do not fault the influencers for chasing the bag as the young people say. But how proud can you be of putting your bodies and the pranks, and all the buffoonery on display when that is the very thing that many before you fought, protested and died for you to not have to do in order to be respected by your peers and contemporaries in America and the rest of the world? Being a clown on the internet, telling all your business on social media, or saying and doing things that might be degrading and dilute your true abilities and intelligence should not be the goal no matter how much money is offered to do so. When we as African Americans do that, we simply provide people the ability to laugh at us and not with us. And there is a difference.

The internet has a lot of power if used correctly. The ability to start one's own business selling needs and not necessarily wants is a good thing. Anything, when bought in moderation and to satisfy a need, is going to be beneficial to both the buyer and the seller. The buyer gets a good quality product to meet a need and the seller is then able to make a profit and feed their family.

The internet if used to teach responsibly can open up doors for people who may not have access to the best colleges, libraries, and access to people who through their positive influence have real credibility in the subjects that they speak about. It can literally turn a child into a mathematician, an economist, or anything that does not require a true certification or advanced degree.

The internet can teach you how to handle legal matters without always having to hire a lawyer. I have personally saved thousands of dollars in legal fees by simply being able to know how read (**last chapter**) and being able to look things up on the internet that provide me the right information to write a letter, or speak to someone who is trying to take advantage of what they perceive is my lack of knowledge about a certain situation.

The internet allows you to communicate with family members when you are thousands of miles away, be it in your own country or located on the other side of the world. The internet has limitless possibilities if used correctly.

Black Power (is a State of Mind)

We love to use the internet to follow other people's lives as if we are not capable of having our own lives, and tell our own success stories, and create our own legacies. Be careful of following people whose only claim to fame is telling others how to be successful with no real track record of being successful themselves. That is how people end up in powerful positions, controlling the narrative for millions of people who live vicariously through others.

The internet is a good thing, and it offers up opportunities to Black people that did not exist before. You can open up a store on the internet without having a lot of capital (cash) on hand. And you don't have the burden of a lease for space, or dealing with individuals whose may have ulterior motives to sabotage your business or deny you the ability to have a business as has been and is still the case today in America.

So, remember, you need to master the internet, and maximize it's potential to provide you real opportunities to succeed. It is not there to be a place where you live through others, throw money away on games that just keep on taking, nor is it there to capture you in a way that causes you to cease chasing your dreams.

When my wife decided that she wanted to do something that would give her a sense of pride and ownership in having her own business, she started to sell gently used items as she calls them on-line. What started as a whim is now a family business that both she and my son are involved in on a full and part-time basis. It allows her to work from home and it allows him to chase his dream of creating the next big app. And it allows me to write this book and self-publish it without the approval of someone who may not get what I am putting down. Black Power. A state of mind.

Succeed Despite the Odds

In my entire corporate career of some almost thirty years, I never became so comfortable with my co-workers, peers, or managers that I allowed myself to think that my job was anything more than that, just a job. My heart never bled the most recent mission statement, or purpose of the organization or some theme for the month to try to boost results and increase the profits of an organization that did not see me as anything more than a number. An expendable number regardless of my position within the organization. And all it took was a manager to come along who did not look like me and what was a promising career would be quickly derailed no matter how many degrees I possessed or how many retreats or company picnics I "showed my face" at.

We are not able to see the forest for the trees. There are those who think that the forest should only have one kind of tree and attempt to cut down the other trees for fear they may outgrow them and become the more dominant tree in the forest. The quickest way to get laid off in America is to go against the status quo even if the status quo is decimating and ruining a company that has the potential to be a market leader that can make a difference in society as a whole.

We take pride in wearing shirts with logos and knowing all the slogans and statements without valuing the real asset within any company, and that is us, Black people and other minority and disenfranchised fellow Americans. If we all don't show up for work on Monday, and I mean all of us, phones won't get answered, trash won't get picked up, no one will cook or serve the coffee or latte (light on the sugar, with a touch of cream), deliver the paper or do all of the jobs that for the first time as a result of a pandemic are now classified as essential jobs. The resiliency of Black people and people like them is often the difference between a successful company and a failed one.

I am an advocate of being a good, dedicated worker when you take a job. My father taught me if you take a job, and agree to the salary offered, you do what is asked or directed of you as long as it is not illegal, unethical, unsafe, or immoral. If you have the skills and abilities and your resume reflects that, then you should always seek to be employed and not be a burden on society.

Let me be clear, someone who is down on their luck is not a burden to society. They should apply for assistance from whatever government entity or organization that can help them. It is foolish pride to not ask for or take assistance when you have a family to feed or you need to shelter and feed yourself. What we don't want to do is become so dependent on that help that we lose sight of our dreams and goals to be productive contributors to the greater good of society as a whole.

The challenge and the balance you have to find is what is your real goal when you take a job with an employer. It is simple. You learn all you can and build your resume so that you create a marketable asset that others will want to hire. You also should live your life in such a way that you can save 75% of all bonuses and income left over after all bills and expenses have been covered on a monthly basis, without fail. Because you are chasing three things, financial freedom which gives you the other two things, the ability to retire early or start your own business whichever comes first.

Black Power (is a State of Mind)

It is not about being disloyal to an employer, but instead being loyal to your goals. And by the way, don't tell your employer what your long-term goals are as it relates to the three things. Unfortunately, there are people in this world who don't want to see you do well, and that is not about skin color, that is about jealousy and envy. The attitude is quite often enforced by unsuccessful people whose attitude is "If I have to come to work, so do you". Let's change that narrative.

Don't ever talk about your home, finances or show off a new car at work. That is what I call in the workforce the hook. If they think you need the job to keep up your lifestyle, they can treat you anyway they want to. So the next time you think you are impressing your work friends with that new car, or that new watch, or anything that indicates you are indebted to someone, just remember your manager is hearing that and now has full control of your life. Because you need them, they don't necessarily need you.

These are the types of things that Black people are not necessarily aware of. We have always taken pride in showing our success as a way of saying that we are competing with our peers and contemporaries that don't look like us. But if all you are really doing is keeping up with the Jones's then you don't get it. And keep in mind that you are potentially chasing people who are following the same flawed blueprint as you. That is why corporations don't worry about how much they pay you because they know that the market dictates how much money you make and that is driven by our needing that job to keep up appearances.

Your goal is not to impress people who have no control over your career or can move the bar to get you the next position. Those are your co-workers and peers. Your job is to impress the decision makers without sacrificing your ideals, beliefs, and principles that make you the person you are. Gone are the days of having a plantation mentality about work as if you have no other options or anywhere else to go for gainful employment. You work at a job as long as it benefits you professionally financially and most importantly provides work life balance. As soon as it stops doing that, leave and leave on good terms and work out a two-week notice.

If you have a good situation, and you are growing professionally, feel appreciated and are being treated as an individual who is equal to your peers and those above you, go as far as you possibly can in that organization until you reach the three goals. Then part as friends and have nothing but good things to say about the organization.

We as Black people have to balance what is perceived as overt and covert racism with the fact that it is not our company. Diversity and inclusion training without addressing the bad seeds in the company who exemplify these bad behaviors is, frankly, a waste of time. Filing complaints without a group of people to back you up and who can speak to having the same negative experience normally does not result in a positive outcome or the outcome you are expecting.

And if you are not careful, you will blackball yourself in the industry you are working in. Word travels fast, and birds of a feather flock together. Leave before it gets bad and take the new skills you have learned to a company that wants you. Always keep in mind that the only time you get to have real influence over an organization is when you own the company.

I have no regrets about my career or being ultimately paid a salary that only three percent of the world, regardless of color of gender, can say that they ever achieved without being an entertainer or an athlete. I will also share that being Black in a corporate environment where people I worked with did not look like me a high percentage of the time once my career took off was not always pleasant and could be uncomfortable at times.

Folks sometimes forgot I was Black and just assumed they could say and do anything in front of me, even when they were talking about my fellow Black brothers and sisters in a derogatory manner. I never allowed myself to be accepted into that type of rhetoric and made it a point to protect the very people that they took sport in talking about. And that was the toughest part of my job. I did not fit in with the front line, and I refused to be the house servant. I just wanted to be a man, who happens to be Black, chasing the same dreams as my contemporaries and peers who did not necessarily look like me. Black Power. A State of Mind.

Black Power (is a State of Mind)

Black Wall Street – Buy Black

How <u>WE CAN</u> create our <u>OWN</u> Reparations through <u>BLACK BUSINESSES</u>

I spoke earlier about reading and doing your own research and I stand by that because that is how you begin to solve your own problems instead of letting someone else solve them for you. We are currently in an election year, and the conversation about reparations has come up on more than one occasion in the minority community as an agenda item that continues to be near and dear to African Americans, or some subset of the group depending on who you talk to. And frankly it makes for good talk, but I believe it is unrealistic to think that reparations will ever occur in this lifetime or in the future.

And the further along that this country moves, and as time continues to go by with or without us, if we keep harping on this there will be a level of disappointment that frankly I don't want to have for me or my children or their children for generations to come. Again, it makes for good conversation and is a reminder to society of the social injustice and stain that will forever exist on enslaving a race of people, treating them as less than a person, and then somehow convincing yourselves that the right has been wronged by a bunch of laws that did create progress and opportunity but also are constantly being negatively tweaked to ensure that we as Black people don't get full benefit of these laws.

The key to success in this current world and in particular America is generational wealth and financial security. As Chris Rock said, rich people can become poor on a bad financial decision, but wealthy people are wealthy for generations to come. And that is the reason that reparations are such a hot topic every four years. It is not about someone owing us (Black People) something but instead it is about having a fair chance at the opportunities that America has to offer and being able to create our own generational wealth or at a minimum financial security.

I say opportunity because not everyone, no matter the race, will achieve generational wealth, and some will have to work until they retire one day. But that being said, generational wealth allows us to build our own companies, and provide fair wages and opportunities for our people as well as anyone who is qualified to work in the organizations we build. We are a proud people, descended from Kings and Queens who were capable of doing anything. Just look at history and you will see that many of the inventions that have been patented through proprietary rights versus giving credit where credit is due are the direct result of Black People, other minorities, and those who were disenfranchised and took less than fair market price or no price at all for something that went on to make other Americans rich and create generational wealth for their families. Is it fair? No. Is that life? Yes.

We are asking for a level playing field where the rules are the same for all groups and not just those who have the ability to control the agenda and the narrative. We are tired of chasing the carrot, only to be hit with the biggest stick that can be found without taking the tree itself out of the ground. A lot of promises are made, but seldom kept. We see this big cake called capitalism, but all we get are the crumbs of a decent salary and in some cases the crumbs are not big enough to even bother with in the example of a salary that is not a living wage and less than the market's suggested minimum wage.

Black Power (is a State of Mind)

But there is a light at the end of the tunnel. And it is the very thing that we need the most and that is capital. We as African Americans have a lot of this capital, we just don't know it. It took me doing the research for this project to realize that we do have the capital to create our own reparations if left alone to fend for ourselves based on the very capitalistic society that has for far too long held us back or so it would seem. And that is our spending power in America and throughout the world. Anytime a group of people spend over one trillion dollars a year but only spend three percent within their own demographic or race, well that's a problem and may explain why we don't have the generational wealth we are so badly seeking. That means ninety-seven percent of those dollars are not spent in the Black community but is earned by Black people.

The key to creating a Black Wall street is more about concept than it is brick and mortar buildings lining a street along with neighborhoods inhabited by Black people. The last Black Wall Street was in Tulsa, Oklahoma and was burned to the ground by an angry mob in 1921. It is important to know how Black Wall Street came about and how we might do that again in the current era by simply rethinking how we conduct and do business in the Black community.

Greenwood, Tulsa, commonly known by historians as "Black Wall Street" was borne of the belief that Black People could create their own success and create their own opportunities. And it was all started through owning the land that created the town and a basic premise that Black people could prosper if they came together, consolidated their economic resources, and did business within their own community. This allowed the flow of money to circulate within the Black community creating more entrepreneurs and allowing Blacks to gain economic freedom like never before.

This same type of formula was used by Booker T. Washington at Tuskegee when he was teaching young Black men and women how to not only get an academic education but also teaching them vocational skills that would make them assets in their communities that they would return to after graduation. He taught them how to build buildings, make bricks, plant, and grow crops, raise animals which at that time were key skills that could advance the cause of Black people and provide them financial stability in their communities.

We can talk about reparations till the cows come home and complain about "the man" holding us down as a way of avoiding what is at times a way of life rather than a realistic obstacle. There are challenges that are real and many of them have been talked about, but until we can show that we are willing to do business with each other and move the money within our own communities, well, the reparations conversation for me falls on deaf ears. And there will be times that the money flows out the community because we need a supplier, a bank to give us a line of credit, or we need someone who has an expertise that we don't have, YET.

We need to gain that knowledge and mimic it to create our own suppliers, make our own parts, borrow from our own banks, and develop the expertise through further training, READING to learn, and being mentored by those we feel can teach us and are willing to teach us to be independent and able to help ourselves.

We need to pay market price when we shop within our own communities and not look for a hook up that we would not ask for in businesses owned by people who don't look like us. We need to believe in our own qualifications, certifications and expertise without validation or needing a second opinion that we do not ask for when we do business with those who do not look like us.

Black Power (is a State of Mind)

We need to go to school and become doctors, lawyers, teachers, plumbers, electricians, contractors, agricultural experts and creators and builders of things. When those businesses become successful, we should not "sell out" for a large payday thinking we will continue to run the business or control our product the same way when we owned it.

We need our own record labels, radio stations, and television networks. Again, one trillion dollars can do a lot in the Black community. We have given up so much of what made us who we are that we are slowly losing our own identity. And all for money that obviously is not going back to the very communities that supported these businesses when no one else would.

As a child growing up, I saw my own version of Black Wall Street in the town I grew up in. During the sixties and seventies, the cleaners in my section of town was black owned as was the realtor, the barber shop, the local convenience store, the daycare that I attended until I went to the first grade, the auto mechanic who fixed my dad's cars and the gas station where we all washed our cars on a Saturday prior to hanging out on Saturday night. We took pride in our neighborhood and the businesses took pride in treating their customers right.

I understand those businesses were the products of segregation and therefore there was no choice but to build our own businesses to service a community that was underserved and in some cases not allowed into establishments owned by people who did not look like us. As soon as integration occurred, we packed up, moved to the suburbs, and started doing business somewhere else. And in our quest to prove that we had been given equality and freedom, we abandoned the very businesses that had supported us when others would not do business with us at all. That attitude is still taken today given the small amount of money we spend in our own communities.

Black Power (is a State of Mind)

When one looks at immigrants who come to America, they follow the model that Blacks had no choice but to follow during Jim Crow and segregation. They not only shop at the more traditional businesses, but they also build businesses and shop within their own communities as well. And you know where they are as they are consolidated into certain areas and in some cases spread out, but they cater to a certain demographic and do well as it relates to being a profitable business.

We can and must do better. Our issue is not the need for reparations. We just need to pool our resources, come together to plan, and engage in economic prosperity for our communities that will allow us to build our own generational wealth. And while this is not simple, it is not beyond our level of intelligence or expertise. And there are enough of us with accumulated wealth to jumpstart such a "pie in the sky" program that is not a dream deferred to quote Langston Hughes but instead a dream come true with the right people and more importantly the right attitude about who we are as a people.

The last thing we need to work on is power tripping and wanting to get credit. The quickest way for a business to fail is if the partners become power hungry and worried about who gets the credit or said differently who's the leader and who has to follow. The leader should be the most qualified of the investors to run the business or the collective group should recruit someone to run the business on their behalf.

As for the power tripping part, if you know that you don't have the skill set to do something, but have the money to invest, then don't worry about your role or your title nor should you ask about either. Be concerned about outcomes that grow your investment. And rather than worry about who gets credit for making the business successful, be concerned about building your net worth to help grow a business.

Being an investor is not a bad thing, nor is accepting a role within an organization that you know will be fair and treat you as a valued employee. Bring back Black Wall street. We can do it. Black Power. A state of mind.

The lesson that my mother taught me in this has always remained the same, and I have tried as best I can to teach it to others. I have always felt proud, whenever I think of the incident, that my mother had strength of character enough to not be led into the temptation of seeming to be that which she was not-of trying to impress my schoolmates and others with the fact that she was able to buy me a "store hat" when she was not. I have always felt proud that she refused to go into debt for that which she did not have the money to pay for.

Booker T. Washington
Up From Slavery

Avoid the Shiny Shit – No One Really Cares!

When I was growing up as a child, the most exciting thing in the world was when the Sears Roebuck catalog came to our house. It typically would arrive in the months preceding Christmas; I would like to say it was right before Thanksgiving. That was one of the most exciting times of my life. I would look at that catalog for hours and dream of having everything in it, the toys, the clothes, the shoes, everything I wanted to see under the tree come Christmas. I really thought I was hot stuff. My father would always bring me back to earth about my dreams, my expectations, and our economic reality.

He would tell me the stories of being a depression era Black boy and what he received for Christmas. Although he died and has been gone for over twenty years now, I remember the story like it was yesterday. He would tell me that all he and his sisters and brothers received for Christmas was some pecans, walnuts, and fruit, typically apples and oranges. If he and his sisters and brothers happened upon their "gifts" prior to Christmas and ate them in advance of the holiday, well they would have to take a whooping from my grandmother and a tongue lashing from my grandfather. So that story would always reset my dreams, level set my expectations, and create a reality about what Christmas was really about. It was not about the gifts but instead living to see another Christmas and enjoying family, friends and celebrating the birth of Jesus.

Once the expectations were reset, my father would always tell me to identify my list of the things I really wanted and then place a special mark by the item that I wanted more than everything else. And while that may sound strange and outdated to the current Christmas celebrations, it meant everything to me. Because typically all I received was my favorite thing with the special mark, and maybe one other thing that I had circled.

I remember the year that I got the new Evel Knievel action figure with the motorcycle you would wind up and watch him go. This was around the time he was at his peak and had either jumped or was preparing to jump Snake River Canyon. And then there was the Pittsburgh Steeler letter jacket that I and all my friends wore all day on Christmas to display our favorite teams. I will never forget the year that I received my first Schwinn Carolina Blue ten speed bike. I was hot shit, and in time I could ride with no hands and pop a wheelie from one streetlight pole to the other. My point here is those gifts had sentimental value to me.

Today the young kids wear and have so many clothes and tennis shoes or sneakers that they can put on a different pair based on color to coordinate with their jersey, tee shirt, or polo shirt. And the shoes are multicolored and designed like the fashion items they have become. And yet I can remember begging my father for a pair of leather Nikes when Nike first came out, and he compromised with me and brought me the canvas ones. My disappointment was non-existent because he made the attempt to at least make sure I had some Nikes like the other kids in junior high school. It was when I was in my fifties that I brought a pair of the very leather Nikes that I did not get as a kid from a local Goodwill store and that was more to honor my father than it was to make up for not having them in junior high school. Yep, those were the days. Life was simple, and we did not worship things and all the shiny shit as I call it.

I grew up, my mother and father folded up their tents and went home to GOD, and I got married. I swore that I would always have anything my money could afford, and I would not put parameters on my children so they would always have the biggest Christmases and all the gifts money could buy. As much as I thought I learned the lesson my father and mother were trying to teach me, I chalked up our Christmases and the limited giving to their lack of financial resources versus them trying to teach me one of life's lessons that come with age and wisdom about good fiscal responsibility. To him who much is given, much is expected.

What I found over time is that the pressure to deliver on these extravagant Christmases created credit card debt that lasted well past Christmas and often until I received a bonus from work or my tax refund check. Christmas became so much about gift giving that we lost sight of what Christmas really meant to us, and that was the birth of Jesus Christ, the best gift that Black folk received when they were enduring the oppression and brutality of slavery. If they did not have anything else, they had GOD and for some reason that is bigger than this book or this chapter of the book. That was all they needed.

This is not an agenda on Christmas but instead a narrative on what has happened to us as a people and our warped sense of reality and what defines us as a people. We went without for so long that we began to see life in a perverse way as it related to what is important to us and what wasn't. We became more enamored with the things, and less concerned with honoring GOD and fellowshipping with our loved ones and friends. Over time, Christmas became about the gifts and the worship of getting as much as we could to satisfy a want versus a need so much so gifts sit in some homes today that have not been played with, or worn and before you know it they are being given away to Goodwill or regifted to prepare the closet or toy box for the next Christmas.

We have become so concerned with having things, material things, that we will sacrifice our retirement plans, our ability to save, college funds for the future of our children to live for right now. We will pay hundreds of dollars for shoes that can't read, write, or add. Hell, they can't even make you a better athlete although there are those that think they can without putting in the work required to be a great athlete.

We wear the shoes of a famous athlete but hardly ever live up to the hype and reputation of that athlete, because well frankly, you are not that athlete. We put other men's names on our backs and pay a hefty price to do so allowing our children to look up to the athlete instead of the man or woman who purchased the jersey. I am not knocking being a fan or buying the sneakers or the jerseys, I am questioning the message it sends to our kids. As Charles Barkley so eloquently said, he is not your role model. He was right, we as Black parents should be the role models for our children.

Then there is the amount of debt and the lengths we will go to keep up with our neighbors who are in return trying to keep up with us creating this vicious cycle that no one can afford, and everyone is delusional about. All for some shiny shit.

We drive cars we can't afford, buy houses we don't need but want, and take trips that our budgets can't afford just to go somewhere else and spend five days sleeping, eating, and maybe enjoying the sights and sounds of wherever we are. We don't do these things necessarily because we can afford it, we instead do it because we feel we have something to prove to ourselves, our friends, and to the world to show that we as African Americans have made it. And to the extent that we really can't afford to do these things, well that's a bunch of bullshit.

The pandemic really brought this to light when there were luxury cars sitting in lines for the food bank as people were trying to feed their kids because they had not set aside anything for an emergency. Nothing saved for a rainy day, just living life to the fullest with no thoughts of hard times, a job layoff that lasts longer than expected, or a pandemic that wiped out jobs and businesses that were totally dependent upon this same viscous cycle of spend, spend, spend and figure out how to pay for it later. There are no endless wells of money or financial opportunity for most of us. Not the top one to three percent, but most of us. Because most of us who have to work for a living, may not ever make six figures and need to be disciplined to save first and spend later.

I want you to think about something, how much time do you typically spend in a car Monday through Friday. With the longest commute on average of let's say an hour both ways, that is two hours in a twenty-four-hour day. So, we spend less than ten percent of our time in our car(s) Monday through Friday. But I wonder what percentage of our take home pay is going to car payments, maintenance, insurance, and gas for these same cars. I know without even doing the math that it is a whole lot more than ten percent. Yet we have to have that car. Why do we have to have that car?

Cars give us a false sense of success and create a façade of our lives that don't always relate to our reality. I mean what good is it to drive a BMW or a Benz to an apartment in a neighborhood that the average income does not match the type of car you are driving.

Why would you pay that much for a car when you could be saving for a house instead or using that money to pay for a class, or some training to get you a promotion at work or create a better job opportunity for you? Seriously, who really cares about that car when you drive it to church or to that annual family reunion or college homecoming to try to convince your friends and family that you have it going on.

If they are truly family or dear friends, they should be happy to see you, not what you are wearing or driving. If that's what they are waiting on instead of wanting to see you, I would skip that event next year. And if you have to go out and buy new stuff you can't afford and a car that you don't really need for a weekend event, then you probably should not have gone in the first place.

People who have it going on and are doing well in life don't advertise they have it going on in life. People who are financially secure and have a high level of self-worth don't talk about their net worth nor do they intentionally advertise it. We are trying so hard to be something we aren't, and it shows. I am not knocking wanting to buy things as a reward for your hard work, but I am calling out when we do it just to impress people who either don't care or are going to talk shit about you no matter how hard you try to impress them.

We should stop trying to emulate famous people who are paid to wear clothes, drive cars, and push products on you that they get for free while you pay your whole paycheck to acquire those same products. You can buy the makeup, the clothes, and the cars but you are not them. You are you. Build your own brand and make them buy your brand. If they are not willing to support your brand, why would you every support theirs? Again, we need to invest in each other so that we all succeed.

As I continue to write about Black Power, you will find that our issue is not those who do not look like us, and them somehow holding us back. Instead, it is our belief that we need to emulate someone other than ourselves. The formula is easy. Live within your means, save for the future and for a rainy day, and stop trying to satisfy wants instead of needs for you, your spouse, and your children. Be practical, be frugal and you will always have the things that should matter the most to you. Not material things that you can't take with you.

Build a legacy, generational wealth or at least an inheritance for the next generation and avoid the shiny shit. Black Power. A state of mind.

Reach One, Teach One

No Good Deed Goes Unpunished (and other things I learned along the way)

There is a saying "reach one, teach one" and the intent of the saying is to pay it forward by sharing or teaching something that you know or have experienced with the next person to help them on this journey called life. There appears to be a new attitude of "I got mine, you better get yours" in America in many circles and it does not discriminate or have any social or economic barriers. That attitude is the epitome of selfishness and ultimately allows a few to get benefit of what many need to know and it is also a denial of information that needs to be shared with the next generation. If we fail to share that information, then we set the next generation up for failure.

I like to think that as a writer I am giving back and helping those whose experiences have not been like mine thus providing another viewpoint on how to survive and succeed in America as an African American. One of the best ways to give back is through writing because as I indicated earlier, reading is one of the most important things you can do to succeed in life. A good book may gather dust on a shelf, but the dust comes off when you need pull that book, dust it off, and refresh your memory about something you learned in the past that will help you solve a problem today.

Our youth, young adults and adults entering into the world either after high school or college need guidance. While everyone comes up with this after school program, or youth group, or church group led by someone in the community that actually gives a damn, the finish line is often not reached because the mentor that a child most needs in their life is their parents. Or whomever has taken on the responsibility of raising them and being their caregiver until such time they become adults. That responsibility, while not as critical when they become adults, does not stop because they move out, and start having lives of their own. It is a responsibility that does not stop until you take your last breath.

My first two mentors were my mother and father. Without their guidance, tough unconditional love, and the motivation to see me succeed, I would not be the man I am today. The lessons they taught and shared along with my aunts, uncles, grandparents, and others who helped to shape me, define me, and lay a foundation and blue print on how to be successful in life that is not attained in the streets, at college, or hanging with the fellas. It is the lessons in life that you learn along the way as you grow up and become a man or woman.

I paid attention to my parent's example and how they treated other people, their incredible work ethic, their wanting to help their fellow man or woman, and an unconditional and unselfish approach to parenting that made me know that I was their first priority. Their world revolved around making sure I was doing what I was supposed to be doing and when I got out of line, they had a life affirming way of making me toe the line. I make mistakes to this day, but it does not take much for me to remember a lesson learned, a thought shared, or that look my father would give me for me to know when I was messing up and not being my best me.

It was my mother who tried her darndest at an early age to get me to learn to play golf and the piano. Ultimately, I rejected golf, and played the piano until I was old enough to make it known that I had no interest in playing the piano when all the other guys were at the dust bowl playing basketball. What I did not know then, but I know now is that my mother was trying to prepare me for the life I was growing into, not the life I was currently leading. A life where being well rounded will ultimately keep you from being pigeonholed into thinking society only works one way. And if one is not careful, that thinking of being well rounded will cause some to say you are "acting white" and that has no color or culture attached.

Golf is where deals are done by those with the power, fame, and money. Playing an instrument demonstrates to others that your talents and abilities are not limited. But me being me, I wanted no parts of either until many years later when I figured out how to "play the game" of life. I learned that someone wanting to play golf with you validates you are someone worth talking to. No one wants to spend four hours with someone who has nothing to offer but a fairly decent golf game, assuming you have a fairly decent golf game. They want someone they can discuss world events, business, a problem or challenge they need to solve, or a new way to make money or in some cases change the lives of society.

It was on the golf course that I made friends with a man who changed the trajectory of my career and taught me about the finer things in life. It was on the golf course that I was able to blend in with millionaires and people who did not look like me and hold my own both in conversation and putting together a good enough game to be invited back again. A gentleman once asked me to play golf in 38-degree weather on a Saturday. He had asked my white counterparts to come play and they all rejected him because of the weather forecast. I went out and played with him, and we played through the sleet and rain because he had a great front nine, and well if you know anything about golf, if an amateur has a great front nine, they are going to finish the entire eighteen holes.

It was the same guy who I played golf in those cold conditions that taught me that quality was much more important than quantity, pay sometimes and don't mooch off the richest guy in the room, and don't be jack of all trades and a master of none. He taught me that and more. He is the only white man who truly took an interest in me as a person, and not the color of my skin. If not for this man, I would never have lived a life that is only afforded to a few unfortunately and I will always be forever indebted to him for that.

And then there are the mentors who taught me about life in general. There is the aunt who taught me "night has no eyes" which was a warning that in the dark, no one sees what happens to people so be careful. It was my other aunt who taught me "book sense without common sense is nonsense". It was my uncle who taught me that the best job is the job you can retire early from and draw a pension. It was my dad who taught me that when you fall, you get right back up, and never fall intentionally as that means you knew what you were getting yourself into. My father also taught me to have compassion and empathy for others and humble myself because all the college education in the world can't replace treating people the way you want to be treated.

It was a manager at a bank I once worked at who taught me that no good deed goes unpunished as a way of treating everyone the same, and never playing favorites. I learned so much from so many people over my career, some of them not necessarily mentors but people who I respected enough to listen to, regardless of their age, race, or whether they reported to me or I reported to them. But given I could learn something from them, it is fair to say I felt mentored by them to help me be a better person and become successful in life.

In today's society, we let so many of the wrong things and the wrong people teach us, define us, and tell us who we are. Those are not mentors; those are just people we listen to because we don't know the difference between bullshit and real talk. Bullshit is something that if you listen close enough has no substance or quality about it. Real talk is a conversation that resonates with you personally, and you can identify with what you are hearing enough to want to make a change or take a new direction in life based on some value add that has been shared with you. You easily know the difference. All you need to do is consider the source. Black Power. A State of Mind.

Give Back _ It's really not about you!

While I have been extremely successful in life, I have on more than one occasion thought of myself as being inconsistent in my charitable endeavors and at a minimum, I wish I had done so much more. There is no particular reason for that as I find great pleasure in helping others. My wife reminds me that I have been more giving than I think when I take the monetary component out of the conversation. Giving is not always based on checks we have written to organizations and individuals or how much we tithed to a church.

What you will learn from this section is that giving comes from the heart, and it is not always based on a monetary gift but instead what you do to help others, that hand up or that reaching out to make someone's day by simply bringing a smile to their face, for whatever reason. Giving back is more a social responsibility than it is a financial obligation in the Black community. Yes, we need to redistribute that one trillion dollars, but we also need to rethink what role compassion, empathy and a true caring for our fellow man plays in our giving back as well.

And giving back can be done at home, in the neighborhood, at school and on the job. As you read this section of the book, many of you will find that you yourselves have been charitable givers again when you remove the monetary component that is not the only form of giving. And that monetary component is at times driven by the tax breaks that come with it rather than the true intent, which is to help others. Which is why the charitable contributions you make in life that have no money attached to them can at times be more fulfilling in making you whole as a person.

Black Power (is a State of Mind)

As a child growing up, we did not have a lot and yet I did not go without any of the basic needs of life either. My parents provided for me, kept clothes on my back, shoes on my feet, and we had heat in the winter and air conditioning in the summer. There was always ice for a cold drink and hot water for a cup of hot cocoa. As I have traveled the world, and these United States, I now know that I should never take these things for granted because unfortunately not everyone can say the same thing. Which makes giving back all the more important.

The most charitable person I have ever had the pleasure of meeting was my own father. And again, he was not a rich man and did not ever have a whole lot. But he gave in such a way that people remember him for being a kind, gentle and compassionate man for all he did to help others.

I can remember him telling me after school one day that we were going for a ride. My father took me with him everywhere he went most of my life as we were never apart except the four years that I was at college. Other than that, I was his riding partner, and for me that was the greatest thing in the world. So, as I tell these stories of giving by my father, understand that I was there each time to see it with my own eyes.

So back to this ride with my father. I get in the car, and ask where we are going, and his famous last words would be we are going for a ride and won't be gone long. Anytime my dad said we won't be gone long; we were typically gone for a long time. He and I got into the car, drove over to his friend's house that lived a mile from us in the same neighborhood and he picked up the adult daughter and we were on our way. Well sixty miles later, and now having passed through two or three small towns, we pull up to a dealership and the daughter gets out and thanks my father for taking her to the dealership.

She had purchased a new car and needed a ride to go and get it. She gets out of the car, and my father proceeds to ask me if I am hungry. We stopped and got a burger and fries and headed back home talking and enjoying the scenery along the way.

Now while I was agitated at first because as a child you just want to go outside and play with your friends (this is when you actually went outside and played with your friends), you could not help but smile when you realized your dad was a pretty cool guy for driving all that way after he had worked all day, not ask for a dime of payment, and then buy you a burger and some fries for keeping him company on the way back home.

And then there is the time that I went to visit my father at work for lunch. My father drove a truck and delivered packages that were of official business on a military base. He and I and some of his buddies went to the diner to get, you guessed it, burgers, and fries. And my father notices that one of his buddies asks for just a water. My father sees this and slides my tray down to his friend. His friend of course tells him he does not have to do that, but my father insists that he take the food. He then tells me that he and I will split a burger and fries. And sure enough, we split the burger and fries and he and his friends have the grandest time talking about stuff hard working men talk about at lunch. And what do I get out of that situation? Learning that a kind heart goes a long way in this world, and you don't always have to have a lot of money to make a difference in someone's life.

I remember my father coming home one day after catching a special at the local grocery store on two-liter Cokes. He must have had ten or fifteen in the back seat of his car. Me and all my friends were playing in the street when he pulled up. I ran over to the car to say hi as I was always excited to see my dad. All the other kids came up to say hi as well and one of them noticed all the sodas in the back seat. I believe it went something like this, "Wow, look at all those sodas!" My father without hesitancy then proceeded to pass all the sodas out to all the kids and told them to take them home for their families. That was not his original intention but that is what he did. I think we ended up with two sodas that day. Ultimately, the sale did not benefit our household, but it sure benefited the neighbors and my father's soul.

I also remember that what seemed like every Christmas for a long while my father would buy a bottle of Crown Royal for every neighbor in our cul-de-sac as a way of saying to all of them thank you for being kind neighbors. Our cul-de-sac had five homes that were facing the street including ours. He never expected anything in return, but always appreciated a thank you when received. That was my dad.

My father did a lot of cooking for folks as he had a reputation for making the best potato pies in town. He always did it on his dime and never asked for any payment. I never remember him ever reminding someone what he had done for them when times would sometimes get hard for him. Nope, he did it, expecting nothing in return. Charity at its best.

There is also the story of the nurse in the hospital who was filling in on the maternity ward and found out a little baby was being put up for adoption to become a ward of the state, what we call foster children today. That same nurse and her husband did not make a lot of money, they did okay and already had a son who was nine at the time and they of course were in their mid-forties. She went home and asked her husband if they might consider adopting this child so that he would have a kind and loving home. And this man without pause told her yes, they should adopt the child and they would figure the rest out going forward. That nurse was my mother and that man was the same man I talked about earlier. Always the givers.

Back in those times, nurses like my mother would get calls from friends to help diagnose a certain condition or ailment, one to save on a medical bill that could be avoided, and two, it was often after hours and the doctor's office would be closed. My mother always tried to help. That's just who she was.

Her greatest gift was to take a child (me) that she adopted and teach him to be all that he could be and never let the color of his skin be a detractor to living out his dreams. And that, my friends, is priceless (so precious it's value can't be determined).

I watched both my mother and my father do so many small acts of generous giving over the years that never required a lot of money, but if a monetary value could be assigned, it would be well into the thousands of dollars of help and labor that they were not paid for and never expected anything in return. And my wife, my children and I have had tried to do the same as well.

The point I am trying to drive home is that there is a lot of work to do in the Black community to make us strong again, and have us be dependent upon each other to revive what was once a thriving group of people who did not ever have a lot, but we had each other. Many of you who read this have no idea what a rent party is. Or know what it means to let someone borrow your suit jacket for an interview or let a friend sleep on your floor as they come into town for the biggest interview of their lives. You don't know what it's like to help a young man or woman get off the streets before the streets take them. Or to let a friend or relative borrow your car for a big interview so they can become less dependent on a system and' create independence for themselves.

We have become such an "all about me society that giving is not something that is top of mind for us. Keep in mind that it does not take a lot of money to help someone. It takes acts of kindness like cutting your neighbor's grass when their lawnmower is in the shop. Or instead of watching your neighbor get evicted from their home so you can talk shit about them, actually giving a shit and assisting them with a few dollars. You would be surprised at the number of people that have been twenty dollars short of keeping the lights on or the cable hooked up. Don't judge the folks having cable, see the bigger picture.

The goal of giving is not to tell folks about it so that you can get credit for it. Or taking a selfie posing as you hand a dollar to a homeless person or bragging about it on the internet via social media to impress your followers, fake friends, or people you have never met to increase your friend number.

Giving is something that is done from within and requires no long thoughts about the implications, passing judgment on those in need or trying to figure out if you can make it a deduction on your taxes. It is a voluntary exercise in compassion and empathy. Many of us hoard money and things that could be used by others while it gathers dust in our homes or will be passed on to a generation that will either screw it up or have more than enough to serve their needs without the excess that could have been used to help someone else.

There is a story in the Bible where a rich man confronts Jesus and indicates that he has led an honorable life trying to do the right thing at all times. Now he wants to know what it will take to be a follower of Jesus, and Jesus makes a simple request of him. Sell everything he has, give it to the poor and follow him. The rich man decides that he can't give away his riches, and promptly leaves.

Give when you can, all that you can, and don't always think of money. Black people have always been a kind, compassionate and generous people dating back to slavery. Many Black people have come before us that sacrificed the blood, sweat and tears poured out on cotton fields, as sharecroppers, living in less than squalor conditions, and who were treated like they were three-fifths a person. It's not about what you don't have, it's about what you can give.

As for giving monetarily to the church or donating to any organization, my only advice there is that you should always hold those accountable who ask for your money to fund an organization, it's charitable giving or any other legitimate reasons for the money. If they can't do that, then you should refrain from giving them money. Don't shortchange your own house to build someone else a mansion. Or to buy them a plane. That's not in the Good Book, or any book that speaks to ethics, integrity and having good morals.

Make a difference in someone's life other than your own. There is a simple thing that we must all remember. We can't take it with us. If a rich man and a poor man dies on the same die, they both die the same way. No longer does their net worth on earth matter. People work night and day to make lists, that determine where they rank in power, or net worth, for a status symbol. No matter what your race, or economic status, you should treat people the way you want to be treated. Period.

All that matters is your self-worth and how people will remember you. I will always remember my dad for his ability to care about someone other than himself. And my mother for making me her son. I can only hope that the people I encountered along the way will say the same about me. Give back. No greater feeling in the world. Black Power. A state of mind.

Teaching Our Children – Their best teacher is you.

One of my pet peeves for the better part of my life has been this attitude of teachers having responsibility for students being well mannered, able to deal with conflict, socially well rounded, as well as being good students academically and athletically if they are inclined to play sports. I have lived on this earth long enough to know that the teachers are not responsible for any of that. Teachers are positive reinforcers of the behaviors that should have been taught by the parents. Not the opposite.

Critical to helping the teachers teach me which was their only job was that my parents did theirs as well. My parents would remind me of their expectations of me as a student of the teacher. *"You go to school to get a good education. Mind your teachers and do what they tell you. Don't talk back and don't make me have to come to school for your foolishness. If I get a call and have to leave work for nonsense that you know you should not be doing, there will be a problem."* Now full transparency I did get in trouble on occasion over my twelve years of school, what I made sure of was that my parents did not get that call. I followed their guidance and advice enough to do well in school and make them proud of me.

My best three teachers during twelve years of school were all African American. They were my fourth, fifth, and sixth grade teachers. Ms. Mann, Mrs. Council, and Mr. Carroll. They all set a great example of professionalism, actually caring about their students, and treated everyone the same no matter the background, street address, or economic status. They instilled and required that we be disciplined students who were engaged in learning. They had easy to meet expectations, yet they pushed us all to be good students. I remember them distinctly because they showed me something about myself that as an impressionable young man

I could not yet see. The foundation they provided allowed me to make mistakes but have the resiliency to bounce back.

Today, there is an expectation that the schools will do what those teachers did for me. Except the rules have changed. They can't discipline like they used to. We have now entered this phase where parents sometimes question the amount of homework being assigned as it is too taxing on the child's personal life. I have seen a shift in the educational system, not driven by the teachers, but those who think they know how to do a teacher's job. The teachers are all educated, know their craft, but are not always given the resources, tools, and free will to teach children the way that works for them individually versus a managed curriculum that sometimes gets in the way of providing what is best for the student.

Schools in some cases push students through whether they have the basic skills or not to function in society. We speak critically of the dropouts, but we very seldom talk about John or Jane who can barely read or do basic math when they get their diplomas. But we celebrate a graduation into a life for these same struggling students as if they accomplished something without regard for how we may have failed them for the rest of their lives.

And if we don't help them or they don't make the necessary corrections to offset that failed education, then a normal life for them becomes difficult to manage, hard to overcome, and when they become adults, they may suffer the repercussions that can potentially lead to poverty, a life of crime, and a straight path to nowhere.

And that is not the school's fault, whether it is in a good neighborhood or a neighborhood defined by some as a bad neighborhood. I personally don't know what a bad neighborhood is because the majority of people, no matter their economic situation, want to wake up and do the right thing every day. For that reason, there are no bad neighborhoods.

Rather than try to change the system, it's time that Black parents create an educational system within the system to ensure that Black children have the best of all worlds. I know this system because I applied it in my own home. From that came two sons who both went to college on full academic scholarships, just as I did when I went to college. My wife and I did not help them with their homework or get in the way of the teachers. We supported the teachers through positive reinforcement of what our sons were being taught at school.

Up until the sixth grade, each year I went to Wal-Mart and bought these books that looked like thick coloring books. They were primers for the grade that my children were going to. Each summer prior to the start of the new school year, I would get the primer for them. Their mother and I would require them to put in at least thirty minutes a day with the goal to have the bulk of the primer completed by the end of summer if possible. It introduced them to the things they might see in the coming year which gave them a head start and also I am sure alleviated a teacher from having to spend extra time with them to understand something they were familiar with versus seeing it for the first time.

We also bought them books, and my wife took them to the library ever week to check out the books of their choosing as well. They also participated in story time where the librarian would read a book to them. I worked a lot of hours back then, so my wife was charged with ensuring they completed their assignments.

Black Power (is a State of Mind)

There will be those that say that having both parents, and us being engaged in their learning provided them an advantage that some Black kids do not have today. To that I say I understand but keep in mind that we did not do the work for them. We required them to do the work. The primers were not expensive, and a library card was free. Those two simple things made a difference in their educations. And our absence or presence was not a deterrent to them putting in the work. The children have to put in the work, plain and simple. Not their tutor, not Google, not a big brother or sister, and definitely not the parents. We can't do nothing, and we should not do everything for our children. They need to put in the work themselves. Period.

And we need to best we can provide a home environment and a space for them to do this work by making sure it is safe, secure, and conducive to learning. Cut the TV and video games off when they are trying to study. Don't allow loud music in the house when they are trying to learn. Provide them an environment that feels like the library and provides them the best chance to succeed at school. And that does not require spending a lot of money. It just requires prioritizing their education and setting the example for them.

I will never forget the day my neighbor, who was Indian, told me that his son had received scholarship offers to study engineering from three of the best engineering college programs in our region of the country. I swiftly went into the house and told my two sons who were I want to say 11 and 9 at the time, that if that young man, whose family had migrated to the United States for a better opportunity, could get a scholarship, so could they. 7 and 9 years later, they both did.

What we as their parents did along the way was support the teachers, provide them the resources and environment to succeed and got out of their way. Many a weekend Sunday or a late-night weekday was spent burning the mid-night oil to study for a test or to get ready for an exam. I knew then what I want you to know now. You can't take education away from a child once given. When that child becomes an adult, their literacy of the basics leads to the literacies required to function in this world, and the understanding that learned individuals have a higher chance at success than the unlearned.

Let me provide some clarification as well around college and what it's true benefit should be. When Booker T. Washington started Tuskegee Institute his goal was to produce students who could function in the world and be both gainfully employed and an asset to society. And that goal should remain today.

We have spent so much time convincing ourselves that a college education is a ticket to the promised land and that is not absolutely true nor is it in any way false. The truth is a college degree is not a guarantee of a bright future and the lack of one is not a guarantee of a bleak life. There are a number of people not playing sports or in the entertainment industry who have gone on to accomplish great things without a college degree. There are those in those two areas who have taken the riches gained from those ventures to form companies, start schools, and provide electricity to people who did not have it previously.

There is nothing wrong with going to junior college or getting trained to be a good electrician or plumber, or brick mason, or painter. All of those skills are necessary, will stand the test of time, and can lead to you having your own business.

The key to life is having a plan. There are myths in the Black community that have to be debunked in order for our young people to get the education needed to be assets to themselves, and their communities. Your parent's past failures or successes don't translate to how your future will be determined. There is generational wealth and that is inherited. There is to my knowledge no such thing as generational failure. We are each uniquely born with our own DNA and brains. Which gives all of us in good health and of sound mind the ability to succeed in life.

We should never allow our children to make up excuses for not succeeding as long as we are not impediments to their success. There will always be exceptions, things beyond their control, and extreme circumstances and events that might impede success. That is not something that should be taken lightly or used as an excuse when it does not exist in reality. Everyone has been through something in life, there are no perfect situations, and the goal is to overcome the obstacles and challenges when they are within our control to overcome.

Parents should not argue the history being taught to your children at school. Don't get into the politics of it or question the intent. Instead, teach your children the history you want them to know but balance that with both their ages and their ability to handle what they learn from you and what is taught to them at school.

There should be a concerted effort to have them learn Black history as soon as possible providing autobiographies, and historical information that will give them an appreciation of who they are as Black children. The goal is to get them to appreciate all who came before them, what they went through to get us to this point, and the debt that is forever owed to ensure that the history and the people associated with it are never forgotten.

It is not about teaching the oppression or painting a picture of a people who gave up, but more about teaching them the successes and accomplishments of our people that may never show up in a classroom. Have them understand the importance of knowing how to read and write and the fact that we were in this country for over two hundred years before we began to learn to read as a people.

Have them learn the history of the HBCUs (Historically Black Colleges and Universities) and why an education from an HBCU will stay with them the rest of their lives. If they are going to go to college, there are good HBCUs with reputations of graduating outstanding engineers, doctors, lawyers, and business leaders all over this country.

And let me make this point truly clear. Before any mainstream institutions would admit us given our lack of education previously and right after slavery, it was HBCUs that gave us an opportunity to be college graduates and assets to our local communities. Booker T. Washington, the founder of Tuskegee was a graduate of Hampton University. W.E. Dubois was a graduate of Fisk University prior to graduating as the first African American to receive an Ph.D. from Harvard in African American Studies. Martin Luther King, Jr. was a graduate of Morehouse. Thurgood Marshall was a graduate of Howard as is Kamala Harris, our current candidate for Vice President. Spike Lee and Samuel L. Jackson are both Morehouse men.

There is a stigmatism about HBCU's that permeates through the Black community and supported unfortunately by many of our own people that that education is less than a mainstream education and will make our children inferior in the workplace bland affect their income potential. And yes, there are people who will judge them on that. I am a graduate of an HBCU, and when all was said and done, I was making more money at my peak annually than a significant number of my male counterparts, regardless of race or where they went to school.

I make it a point to reflect silently on my success and earning potential when they profess to be smarter than me or frown upon my educational background. Bottom line in this capitalistic society is we are graded on our ability to earn a good income, and I was in the top three percent of all Americans, and the top 1% of African Americans. So, tell me how a degree from an HBCU hurt me? Because it did not. It is my opinion that an HBCU will prepare a Black man or woman for the real world, no matter where he or she goes to graduate school afterwards.

And if your child is an excellent athlete, provide them the opportunity to visit at least one HBCU for every mainstream institution. It is important that they understand that it does not matter where they go to school. If they have the talent and the ability, the pro scouts will find them. Just ask Darrel Armstrong, Shannon Sharpe, Doug Williams, Jerry Rice, Steve McNair, Everson Walls, Al Attles, Walter Payton, and many other Black athletes who went on to have long pro careers from HBCUs and make the Hall of Fame in their respective sports.

Let them read anything and everything they can get their hands on about us as a people, our inventions, our speeches, and all the creative and innovative things that we were able to do over the past 400 years. It is important that our youth understand they are the future and always have been. Teach them to believe in us as a people, and by default they will believe in themselves.

Wakanda is a state of mind for our people. It is not a fantasy about a Black superhero. It is our reality. All we need to know is our history and it becomes noticeably clear that we are not inferior, nor do lack certain cognitive abilities to be anything we want to be. What we need is a renewed vision, a short- and long-term plan for success, and good mentors for our children. All of that comes from you, the parent, the best mentor(s) a child could ever have.

Take charge of your child's education, don't depend on a system to do for your child what you can do for them. Don't pay for 100 television channels, pay for the best internet. Don't buy expensive tennis shoes, buy books that will be with them forever. Don't take them to the mall, take them to the library. And reward them for hard work. Need money for anything? Do your homework, get good grades, and be well mannered and productive. And then we will talk. Black Power. A state of mind.

Black Power (is a State of Mind)

Politics and the Black Community

Why we need to VOTE!

Politics in the black community is an awkward state of affairs. There is no easy way to write this part of the book but to just dive right in and try to be politically correct while making us, as Black people rethink politics and what it really means to us. Politics is polarizing, no longer is it bipartisan on the most important issues that affect the greater good of the majority of the people and frankly, I am completely turned off by the whole process.

But having said that, we, the Black Community, need to and should always vote! It is the most powerful political tool we possess to affect potential outcomes and laws that benefit us. We are only thirteen percent of the population but when it is time to vote, our thirteen percent has shown time and again that we can be difference makers. Just ask Barack Obama.

Politics by one definition I read is *the activities associated with the governance of a country or other area, especially the debate or conflict among individuals or parties having or hoping to achieve power.* In the past few years and decades, it has become less about governance specifically at the national and state level, and more about the latter of parties having or hoping to achieve power.

All one has to do is look at divide that exists between the Republicans and Democrats to understand why it is such a turn off. I did not know politics would require you to represent your party's ideals exclusively or you are not considered worthy of or reliable enough to have an opinion. Until someone told me that being an Independent means you are not reliable, and you don't represent anything. And it has become for the average American who depends on politicians to govern the country, their state and local municipality a conundrum of sorts to understand what is being done in their best interests versus the interests of the most wealthy and powerful of us as citizens. The lobbyists in D.C. outnumber the congressmen and the interests of a few individuals appear to outweigh the interests of the people as a whole.

Politics has never offered a perfect solution for everyone involved no matter what party you affiliate with. The difference now is there are some fundamental concerns and challenges that are negatively affecting minorities, the disenfranchised, and the poor. Those same groups who can feel marginalized at times do not have the ability to influence ultimately the laws and programs that can at times appear to reward a select few and feel punitive to others. All they have is their vote and that is why voting rights and their proper enforcement are so critical. There are certain ideals about this country that should not have a party associated with them.

Free speech, the right to bear arms, the ability to vote in a fair and equitable election, being fiscally responsible, and taxing everyone equally should not be about party. Taking care of our infrastructure, paying our teachers, police, and all hard-working people a fair and equitable wage should not be about party.

Providing the opportunities to all individuals to succeed and live the American dream should not be about party. Eliminating racism in common environments that we all utilize, need or work in should not be about party. Having a strong military should not be about party.

And then there is the biggest elephant (no pun intended) on the table and that is capitalism. Capitalism should not be a dirty word that is the opposite of socialism. Capitalism in a fair and responsible democracy should be wanted and accepted by all Americans, regardless of party, race, or current economic status.

Everyone who aspires to should have the ability to start the next great company and their economic success should not be frowned upon nor should there be an expectation that the owner(s) give more than their fair share to a society that did not build the company, but expects that there is debt owed to them by the person who founded the company.

The founder and owner should want to do the morally correct thing and pay his or her people fairly, sell their product at a fair price based on the market, and be able to make a profit without any constraints that limit their ability to be as successful as they want to be. You can't expect someone to build something from scratch, be remarkably successful at it and then somehow feel like they owe you something. That is called an entitlement and for-profit organizations have no obligation to provide entitlements to people who did not build the company.

So, there you have it, and believe me, the complexities of society, politics, and government are many and there is no one person that has all the answers for all the people all the time. What one should hope for is that all politicians at all levels of government do a fairly good job of balancing the needs of all the people with the ideologies of the people who put them in office, and that is not just the voters but the people whose interests, politically and financially influenced who was finally voted into office.

One of the challenges that many Americans have, specifically African Americans is that the government is somehow going to solve many of our problems and challenges. What we as African Americans need to realize is that there are some common problems and challenges that are not just conducive to African Americans but all Americans. There are educational, infrastructure, and healthcare issues just to name a few in all communities. And while our challenges are real, we must understand that candidates can't have a Black agenda, so we need to stop pushing that narrative every four years when it is time to vote in a new President. What we should expect is that they recognize that there are some inequities that need ongoing dialogue and where appropriate the introduction of or the changing of laws to create equality and fairness for all Americans.

The reparations conversation is dead on arrival because it has no teeth to it. There are far too many congressmen, mayors, police chiefs, athletes, entertainers, authors, musicians, business leaders, millionaires, and a few billionaires in the African American community to keep saying that somehow, we have not advanced enough so therefore we are owed some type of financial stipend.

Unfortunately, reparations should have been done during reconstruction, and it should have been done in a way that it was a recorded event in history with documentation to explain what was given and how it was given. To try and prove who dates back to slavery and drawing straight lines in the sand to prove ancestral relationships is almost impossible at this point. Not totally impossible, but extremely difficult at best. I appreciate the conversation but again, it is a conversation that goes nowhere fast.

As for generational wealth and the implications of America and capitalism, I can't stress enough that all we have to do is redistribute the over one trillion dollars spent in the Black community to have it circulate within our own communities and we can create our own wealth and lobbyists. Then can we have a greater influence on what laws are passed that directly benefit us as a people. And even then, our goal should be to influence laws that benefit all Americans, not just Black Americans.

We are not and should not ever come across as people who require some type of special entitlement from the government to help us to succeed. What we need and should demand is a level playing field where the programs and financial incentives benefit us the same way they do any other demographic in this country.

We should meet the same standards for qualification for government programs, jobs, and institutions of higher learning, and then we should be given those opportunities based on a merit system that selects the best and brightest, regardless of race.

Until that happens, then yes, we should demand that there be a proportionate amount of resources set aside for us to benefit from the same programs as our counterparts of all other races who are granted access to these programs.

We also need to be smart about our vote. There is no automatic stipulation that we must all be Democrats because of some laws passed fifty plus years ago that made a significant impact on the Black community. That is the equivalent of someone giving you something you should have had anyway and then making you feel indebted to them the rest of their life. We appreciate all laws that have been passed to create equality and opportunity for African Americans, and if we trace our history beyond the sixties, we will find that things were also done for us by Republicans.

We should also want to join the Republican party to influence their ideologies, beliefs, and their agenda as well. We are a big block of voters who typically show up when it counts. That kind of political capital should not be taken lightly. The

Republican party does not exclude us. This is America, you can belong to any party you want. But you need to research the ideologies and philosophical beliefs of the party and then look at your own values to see where you best align.

And you may find that you are an Independent because you align with things that are important to you in both parties. You may also find that you have more in common with Republican ideals than you think. Not a candidate for election, but the beliefs of the party they represent.

And don't vote a certain way because that is what the previous generations did. That is a debt that is not owed, and if it was owed, well that's confusing again, because a Republican freed us, and Democrats gave us Civil Rights and Voting Rights. This will be controversial for those who want to stir the pot, but for those of us who think for ourselves, well the decision to be who you are is well, your decision. I don't personally vote for parties, I vote for individuals who align with my beliefs or in some cases who I feel can do the best for the most people, regardless of racial or economic status. That is what a democracy is to me.

Your vote is your vote, and you should do what is in your best interests first, then the interests of the majority of the people, not a subset of people. Because if you are trying to do what is only in the interest of Black people, then if you are not careful, you are mimicking the very thing that we scream about the most, doing something for one group while excluding the needs of all groups. No easy answers here, but you want to air on the side of what is best for Americans, all Americans and by default Black Americans will benefit as well. Black Power. A state of mind

Black Power (is a State of Mind)

Dear Kings and Queens

Inheriting the Crown

The next section is a letter to the future African American Kings and Queens. They are currently our Princes and Princesses. They are all between the ages of 16 and 35 and the future of the Black community rests squarely on their shoulders.

They will define who we are, what we become, and how far we go or don't go. They are our future.

I write this letter at this time because I worry about the extinction of the Black man and woman, not in the physical sense but as it relates to our culture. I worry that we will continue to lose our identity through forgetting who we are and where we come from.

It feels at times, and I have had my own doubts as well, that we have lost everything that defines us as a people. Our music, our neighborhoods, our elderly, and the wisdom that they imparted on many and most of us, our lifestyle, our dance, even our facial and physical appearance. Much of that has been hijacked and coopted by so many that it is extremely easy to see someone who for lack of a better term is "acting Black."

The next generation needs to redefine our culture, our lifestyle and all that defines us in a way that we don't blend in, but instead stand out as we have for hundreds of years. Much of what we learn and understand about us is what defines us.

Being successful, responsible, and well-mannered is expected. Being "boogie", stuck up and acting as if we are in fact better than those of us who look like us is irresponsible. We have an obligation to each other that if not continued will result in the African American losing site of what makes us uniquely American. I agree that we all want to be seen as Americans and made to feel that there is a level playing field, but we should not forget where we come from, how we got here, and the people who paved the road for us that each year has less potholes for us to navigate around. Black Power. A state of mind.

Black Power (is a State of Mind)

Dear Future Kings and Queens,

It is with a heavy heart and unbridled optimism that I make this appeal to you as the future leaders of the Black community to consider greatly the letter that I am writing to you. I chose your age group (between 16 and 35) because you are the future. You are the big brothers and sisters, the new parents, the first in your family or the second generation, you are the creators of startups, hall of famers, you are the religious leaders we so strongly need right now. You are the past, the present, and the future.

You have had access to the whole world and have been able to make inroads into a society that for over two hundred years physically enslaved those who came before you. And then for a very brief period of time Black people were set free or so it seemed through the Emancipation Proclamation only to be mentally enslaved for another one hundred years. There appeared to be a light at the end of the tunnel, and it was called integration. And it worked and continues to show progress for you and those who look like you. Except for one thing.

This integration of us a people actually segregated us to some degree all over again. It took the best and brightest of us and sprinkled us all over this great country called America and left behind a neighborhood that became "the hood" and left many of us behind to fend for ourselves. Those of us who made it remain segregated in a lot of cases. We just are allowed to live in a better house and send our children to a better school.

We just want to blend in and fit in even if that means we completely renounce our culture, our dress, who we name ourselves to avoid being profiled on a job application, where we go to school, and how we conduct ourselves in front of people we feel the need to impress even when that is not necessary.

The most successful of us are segregated in our own neighborhoods from folks who don't want us there and we are segregated from our own people because frankly, once we leave the hood, very few of us make regular trips back. The fear of so many things that are real to us keep us from going back. We leave our own people behind while we move forward to a life that is meaningless without knowing who we really are, and that is Black Royalty.

We are trying so hard to be accepted by people who to my knowledge have not rejected us. As a matter of fact, a significantly high percentage of them don't demonstrate or show any ill will towards us. They go about their daily lives just as we do. In my fifty plus years on this earth, I have never been called a nigger by a person who did not look like me. I have never been called a boy, nor has anyone made me say Yes Sir or Yes Ma'am to them other than when I served in the military and there it was expected of everyone, not just those of us who happened to be Black. Have I been treated differently on occasion because of my race in the workplace? Absolutely. Did it stop me from being successful? No. And why is that? I am glad you asked.

There is an expectation of all people, regardless of racial or socioeconomic background, to conduct themselves in a manner that is professional, gains respect, and makes them a productive member of society. There is an expectation that you maintain a high level of ethics and integrity which demonstrates that you will treat others fairly and in the way you would want to be treated. And that is not acting like one race or denying the race you belong to. That is just doing what's right to make the world a better place.

There is a further expectation that while you will make mistakes in this journey called life, you learn from them and try not to repeat them over and over again. To do the same thing over and over again and know that it is wrong is the epitome of not caring about yourself or those who care about you. To have complete disregard for your fellow man and to want to intentionally cause them harm either mentally or physically is well, selfish and shows a level of ignorance to who you are and the baton that is being passed to you to carry your people forward.

What is needed now more than ever is leaders who can set the example by demonstrating during every waking breath that you are trying to make a difference in this world, a positive and influential difference. Not a fifteen minutes of fame difference. Not a selfie difference. Not a false sense of security difference as a result of having followers who know nothing about you other than you are famous for being famous. Better to have changed a small part of the world than to be known by the whole world while lacking anything that can change the world and make it a better place.

Now I know this feels like a lecture and that's exactly what it is. It is a lecture that has been long overdue. People have told you that you are smart all your life. They have given you participation trophies and certificates for doing what you are supposed to do as if you have accomplished something.

You have been given expensive shoes, clothes, cars, and the latest gadgets that were not always earned, but given to you so that you could keep up with some friends that don't necessarily challenge you to be your best you but instead try to influence you to follow the same people they follow so you can all be followers of somebody whose relevance again is being famous for being famous. And if you think about it, if all you are is a follower, when do you ever become a leader?

And the Black community needs leaders in all walks of life right now.

We have an epidemic of sorts of trying so hard to be something we aren't and working diligently to be accepted as a follower that we have forgotten how to be leaders. I have watched hundreds of thousands of people march for us and with us which is commendable. What I did not witness or see was the leader or leaders who came forward with a real agenda for Black people. It's cool to put on a black outfit, a black mask, and scream Black Lives Matter and I support the intent and the effort.

My question is where is the real agenda? And that is bigger than wanting to defund the police or call the brothers and sisters in blue, many of them being people of color and in quite a few cases Chiefs of Police racists by virtue of a uniform they proudly wear just like the military uniform I wore and my father wore before me. As you pay attention to what is going on around you, ensure that people who you are supposed to trust with your future are not feeding you propaganda that fits their political agenda and has nothing to do with your real agenda, fairness and equality for all. There are bad apples in every organization, but that does not make the organization bad.

And this epidemic is made further difficult by what has become the new crack cocaine for Black America and to a greater degree all of America and the world. These gadgets that we all carry with us 24 hours a day are dumbing us down, making us numb to real world issues, and tearing down the very culture that we so badly need right now to understand who we are as a people and why we must hold each other accountable to ensure that we don't become extinct as a race of people who have struggled with having an identity for most of our lives spent in this foreign land that we learned to call home called America.

You are a generation of bright intelligent people who long to belong to something that will make you feel whole. You want to be accepted, exalted, and have it given to you without putting in the work. You would rather be famous for being famous than to be known for being a difference maker and a change agent for your people.

Having a bunch of followers for buffoonery and pranks that are done at the expense of a true friend or a girlfriend or spouse is not a value add to you, the person(s) doing it with you or society as a whole. It makes for good laughter but just know that they are not laughing with you, they are laughing at you and that is the difference. It took me some time as a young man to know that I was not funny if I was making a fool of myself. If you tell a joke and someone laughs with you, you are funny. If you tell a joke and they laugh at you, then you become the joke.

There are no shortcuts in life. Having a killer cross over or being able to run a 4.2 forty is great and more power to you. But if that can't translate to a real career in sports that will give you at a minimum a good college education and at a maximum a long pro career; then so what. Don't underestimate the work that MJ, King James, Renaldo, Tiger, Steph, Dak, Ezekiel, Patrick, Lisa, Candance, Serena, and others put in before they made it look easy. You think that if they can do it, so can you. Well look around you.

Using the NBA as an example, there have been a lot of good players in my fifty years of watching pro basketball. But the athletes I remember the most are the ones whose stars were brighter on every stage they stepped on. And when you consider those whose stars were the brightest, the list gets really short. Magic and Larry, MJ, Kobe, and Shaq, and Lebron and Steph.

That is because they played on a level that was unmatched by their peers who were exceptionally good players, some great players but not on the level of these guys. Those seven players have appeared in 32 of the past 40 NBA finals. 80% to be exact. And yet they make up hundreds of players who have played in the past 40 seasons. Or less than 1%. That is why they have been the true leaders of the sport and the most recognized names in the sport. Hard work. But I digress.

Leadership is not hard to do. It does not mean always stepping out front or taking the podium because you are a great orator. Leadership is what you do every day to set an example for those around you to be better and challenge you to be your best. Leadership is getting up early, making your bed, taking out the trash, saying Yes Ma'am and No Ma'am, having respect for your elders and bringing out the best in you every chance you get.

Leadership is not addressing your elders disrespectfully by calling them by their first names versus Mister or Mrs. Jones. Leadership is listening to what the so called "old heads" and "boomers" have to say because they have traveled down roads you have not yet seen and come back from the dark alleys of life that the average person would have never survived on their best day.

They have seen life at its best and they have seen life at its meanest. Not because they necessarily wanted to but because well that's life. The knowledge they can share with you about life's winding path, and the road not always being straight and smooth could be the difference between you living or dying, doing twenty-five to life, or being set up by your co-worker(s) to take a fall that ultimately leads to you being black balled for life. Yep, those that came before you have a lot to offer.

You can learn from anyone. You can learn from a homeless person on how to avoid becoming homeless because no one intentionally becomes homeless. Life has presented some challenges and obstacles that led to the homelessness. You can learn from someone who filed bankruptcy how to avoid becoming bankrupt by listening to them tell you about the poor financial decisions they made in life. I am not advocating or condoning homelessness or bankruptcy because I know from being around people I care about what these things can do to people and I have seen these same people rebound, learn from their past and go on to have productive and successful lives. They were members of my immediate family.

Stop chasing your fifteen minutes of fame. It's not worth it. If you can only be famous for fifteen minutes, you were never famous. You were a scrolled blip on someone's screen who discussed you for about ten minutes, and twenty-four hours later, you were already forgotten. Chase longevity, chase legacy, and chase relevance. You want to be relevant, not famous. There are plenty of famous people in history who are no longer relevant. There are relevant people in history whose legacy is the work they put in; not how many people knew them at the time.

Future Kings and Queens, it is time you think more of yourself than objects and one-word nouns that won't stand the test of time. Influencers, rappers, activists, podcasters, and any other slick new name that means something in the streets. For now. Instead you should want to be artists (who happen to rap), change agents (who make a difference through their activism), leaders (who influence people by providing something of value), and newscasters (who fact check and provide relevant information that can actually be used in a society so obsessed with information that fake news is accepted nowadays more readily than real news).

And before you can do any of that, you must be students of your respected crafts. Get really good at something, master it and the money will follow. Money doesn't change you for the better, it just changes your zip code.

Stand for something other than chasing a bag. Get a good education, read until your eyes hurt, and learn something about the people you now represent. Know your Black history and stop throwing out the same names you learn every February as some indicator of your wokeness. You know the names, Martin, Rosa, Frederick, Thurgood, Harriet, and Malcolm. Broaden your horizons to include the hundreds of Black people who have done great things in music, the arts, entertainment, athletics, government, education, business and in the religious community as well as social activism for over four hundred years to try to keep the dream alive of us being a free people who can take care of ourselves if given the resources, tools, and opportunities.

Having a lot of money, a nice car, and a big house does not mean squat if you are isolated in your home living in a neighborhood where the people have very little in common with you as it relates to your struggles, what you are going through and what you have been through. We have to come up with a way to revive our own neighborhoods before they get gentrified and price out our elders, and relatives into homes and zip codes they really can't afford.

Your generation has to find a way to challenge each other to address what is becoming another epidemic in the poorest of our communities and that is the black on black crime that is tearing us apart and killing our best and brightest before they ever reach adulthood in so many cases. We are fighting over land that does not belong to us and calling it our turf. For something to belong to you, you need to have a signed deed. If you don't have the deed, then you don't have any turf.

Instead of leaving our communities, why not get a degree in criminal justice and come back and police your own neighborhoods? Be an inspiration to the little ones that the police are not their enemy. Our neighborhoods need good electricians, plumbers, doctors, lawyers, accountants, nurses and any and all professions that will change the hood back to the neighborhood it once was.

We should never become numb to the fact that we are equally responsible for our own oppression at times. And to deny that is to look the other way as a matter of convenience to avoid having the real discussion about what is really one of the root causes of our decline in this great country called America. That is our own accountability for our actions, and what we do every day to raise our standards and move the bar to create our own success.

I have said a lot and you have a lot to think about. Remember, you are the future Kings and Queens. America needs you, Black America needs you and I am depending on you to be leaders, change agents and difference makers. We have more than enough internet overnight sensations whose fifteen minutes of fame will be up in well, fifteen minutes. Black Power. A state of mind.

In Honor of....... My Wife

A Mother Who Cannot Sleep

My wife and I have been married for over thirty years now. For the first 18 years of our marriage, she would sleep every night, like any normal person, for seven to eight hours. And she was the definition of a traditional American mom. She has allowed me to chase the American Dream, to be all I can be. She is a mom who provides unconditional love and balance to the discipline that I have instilled in my two sons so that they would grow up to be the fine, educated young men that they are today.

But then I noticed something when my oldest son went off to college. She started to sleep less, often waking up at three in the morning, and unbeknownst to me, she would just lay in the bed and keep her eyes closed until the sun came up. She would not say anything when this new sleeping pattern first started, but eventually I would find out. And she would not tell me why she could not sleep the whole night and chalk it up to the house being too hot or she was feeling a little off. At times, I would try to rewind the day and think about the things I may have said to her that could have raised her stress level and was that the reason she could not sleep? More often than not, there had not been any arguments and I could not remember anything out of the ordinary that would have triggered her restless nights.

But then my son came home from college for Christmas break one year, and I noticed something. My wife would sleep all night again. I did not say anything, I would just observe going forward. And year after year, whenever my son or our sons came home for Christmas, she would sleep all night the entire time they were home. What I discovered was my wife could not sleep unless my sons were home, and I was home. I did not know that she did not sleep well when I went off to serve my country during Operation Desert Storm.

I did know that she did not sleep well when both of our boys, who are now grown men, went off to college.

My wife did not sleep well because well, she worries everyday about me, and my two sons. And when one of us is not home where she can see us at night, well, she does not sleep well. My wife is not your typical mom. She is an African American mom. And being a Black mom in a country that has oppressed Black women for over 400 years brings a certain stress level that triggers many restless nights and if left unchecked, can induce other medical conditions that have nothing to do with being African-American genetically but instead have everything to do with being an African-American mom, period.

My two sons are both in their early thirties now, and yet she has a list of rules for them that do not apply to all sons in America, but almost exclusively apply to African American sons in America. My sons have not been allowed to go for a run in the neighborhood or walk the dog alone because she is trying to keep them alive. Not safe, alive. My sons cannot walk to the store to get a bag of skittles and a tea because well, she wants them to stay alive. My sons cannot get bicycles and ride through the neighborhood because well she wants them to stay alive. My sons cannot do so many things that make them feel like the little boys they once were versus the men they have become. For the most part, they follow her rules, although they tell her all the time, they can take care of themselves and as grown men, well those rules are broken not out of disrespect but as a normal course of their day. I have raised them to fear no man, and they can take care of themselves. She has always told them to be careful and respect all authorities. And they do that as well.

But now we have a new dynamic, a new worry, but it is a new dynamic with an old stain, one that has existed for over 400 years now. My wife worries about their safety, and unfortunately she most worries about them being in the wrong place at the wrong time, and tragically that involves a simple stop by a man who does not respect the very uniform he wears who has nothing better to do that day than fu$% with a young man who does not look like him because well, he can. When he confronts my son because he is jaywalking, or does not look like the people who live around here, or has a broken taillight, or wants to know is that his house as my son inspects the yard that he just cut for his father who works long hours to afford that beautiful home in that upper class neighborhood where the majority of the people don't look like him, my wife worries that my sons won't know what to do although we both have taught them well.

If they turn the keys the wrong way in their hands, and the reflection of the keys unintentionally creates a blind spot for the man in the uniform, will he yell gun and fire off seven rounds because, well he can. If they go to reach in the glove compartment to get their registration and insurance information, will he yell gun and fire two rounds to the head, well because he just can. If they leave the window of their apartments or homes open, will the man in the uniform shoot first and ask questions later about why a Black man was sitting in his own home just eating some ice cream and enjoying a good movie because he can?

When my son runs through the neighborhood that he just purchased his first home in, and someone calls the police because they think there is a strange Black man in the neighborhood versus a new neighbor, will the men in uniform pull up with guns ready and not see my son has his earphones on and keeps running not out of disrespect or because he is running from them, will they jump out and yell stop, and shoot him because he could not hear them all while some white peer of his runs right by in the same neighborhood and stops to film the whole thing because that is his friend and they had plans to go downtown later and peacefully protest the latest victim of a senseless shooting in a Black Lives Matter march?

Whether America wants to admit it or not, the African American mom has had some worry of some kind for damn near 400 years. Will they take my kids away and sell them to the highest bidder? Will they beat my husband today, because he did not pick enough cotton even if I picked enough for the both of us to hit our quota for the day? Will they kick him as he walks down the street in his suit as he tries to find a new job, and push him on the ground only for him to get back up, say nothing, and come home as if nothing happened only to go out back behind the house, punch a wall, and cry because he is not allowed to be the man his father raised him to be because his mother told him to hold that anger, do what those folks tell him to do, and live to see another day? Not a day has gone by in the 400 year history of the African-American mom that she does not worry about her children and her significant other, but that worry gets amped up when it is a Black male, her son, the endangered species of the American human race who unfortunately is hunted like an animal in the wild simply for being Black.

I am a veteran of this country, served in Operation Desert Storm. My father, who died almost twenty-eight years ago, served in World War II and the Korean war. Between the two of us, we have given over fifty plus years of federal, military, and local government service to our country. He fought for a better life for me, and I served so that my children could have and sustain a better life for themselves. He loved America to the day he died. But we have entered a new era now. It gets harder every day to love a country who does not love you back. And I love my country. But America is a country who keeps my wife up at night worrying about her two sons and her husband because we have moving targets on our backs (literally) that if given the wrong place and wrong time, may not allow us to come home that day or any day going forward.

A country that won't pass simple laws that could make a tremendous difference in the hate and unchecked behavior that puts at risk every Black man in America, regardless of socioeconomic status, educational background, or how well mannered, manicured, or groomed they may be. Racial profiling is not about lifestyle and the type of clothes you wear. Or being in a certain neighborhood that one grew up in and still has family and friends there to this day. Racial profiling is about race. Period.

My wife cannot sleep. She is a GOD fearing woman and struggles to find the strength to pray when she turns on the tv and sees a young man who looks just like her two sons get choked to death by the knee or shot in the back seven times, or eleven times, or stopped and then killed for selling loose cigarettes on the street.

Let me be clear. My wife and I have a high level of respect for every professional police officer who wakes up every day wanting to do the right thing and who puts in the time to get to know his or her community, the people he or she serves, and wants to make a difference in every person's life they encounter.

She is overwhelmed with the shock and awe of seeing a man who has no regard for human life, makes sport of shooting a Black man, all while hiding behind a badge and uniform that he neither respects nor should he be allowed to wear.

Black Power (is a State of Mind)

She wonders about the motive of the people who come around every two or four years and asks for her vote but cannot seem to pass simple police reform laws around background checks, psychological testing, and robust, intensive educational training that lasts long enough to weed out those who are not a right fit for the job, defensive training that involves negotiation, de-escalation of a situation, and only shoot if your life is threatened.

She does not understand why those same people ask for her vote but they can't find a way to pay a police officer a fair wage, and give him some other incentives to live in the community and financial incentives to buy a house in the neighborhood he serves so that he knows the people that he may have to respond to during a non-emergency or emergency call one day for whatever reason.

She observes these "caucuses" who have the power to leverage their votes to force legislation but can't profoundly move the needle on police reform while blaming the other party for the inaction of the entire legislative body. But she knows that while they do not have all the votes, they have enough to influence every piece of legislation and should leverage that to get police reform passed.

I can't give her clear answers when she asks why the people, we elect to office won't act. And because I can't give her clear answers, I then have the same questions myself.

So, my wife does not sleep because she is stressed, concerned, and worried about her two sons, her husband, and every Black man in America. She worries because she is a wife and a mom, and her worry is different. There are some who tell my wife not to worry and try to rationalize this through some statistic that marginalizes the victim and his or her background versus understanding that statistic has no bearing on the root cause of the problem. Creating a distraction to avoid talking about the problem does not help my wife and any of the mothers who deal with this either directly or indirectly on an almost daily basis.

What my wife wants, and what I want for her, is a good night's sleep. And not just when my sons come home for the holidays. She wants a good night's sleep, something that Black Women have not had for over 400 years. And after she can consistently get a good night's sleep, then and only then will she feel finally liberated in a country that, frankly, has never made her feel fully at home.